HIDE YOUR GOAT!

HIDE YOUR GOAT

STRATEGIES TO
STAY POSITIVE
WHEN NEGATIVITY SURROUNDS YOU

STEVE GILLILAND

Advantage®

Published by Advantage, Charleston, South Carolina.
Member of Advantage Media Group.

ADVANTAGE is a registered trademark and the Advantage colophon is a trademark of Advantage Media Group, Inc.

Printed in the United States of America.

ISBN: 978-159932-420-3
LCCN: 2013938339

This publication is designed to provide accurate and authoritative information in regard to the subject matter covered. It is sold with the understanding that the publisher is not engaged in rendering legal, accounting, or other professional services. If legal advice or other expert assistance is required, the services of a competent professional person should be sought.

Advantage Media Group is proud to be a part of the Tree Neutral® program. Tree Neutral offsets the number of trees consumed in the production and printing of this book by taking proactive steps such as planting trees in direct proportion to the number of trees used to print books. To learn more about Tree Neutral, please visit www.treeneutral.com. To learn more about Advantage's commitment to being a responsible steward of the environment, please visit www.advantagefamily.com/green

Advantage Media Group is a publisher of business, self-improvement, and professional development books and online learning. We help entrepreneurs, business leaders, and professionals share their Stories, Passion, and Knowledge to help others Learn & Grow™. Do you have a manuscript or book idea that you would like us to consider for publishing? Please visit advantagefamily.com or call 1.866.775.1696.

I wrote this book for every person who has ever said, "Why me?" It is for all those who feel as if everywhere they turn, they meet problems, obstacles, or difficulties—large ones, small ones, and all sizes. It is for everyone who has ever put up with a nosy neighbor, fickle friend, sneaky sibling, envious family member, scheming coworker, manipulative boss, conniving acquaintance, impolite employee, disrespectful adolescent, hypocritical human being, dishonest subordinate, or people who think the world revolves around them. It is for anyone who struggles to stay positive while dealing with life's disappointments and the negativity that encompasses our society.

While I cannot change the people or circumstances that get your goat, this book is dedicated to everyone who needs help in hiding it.

CONTACT STEVE:

To schedule Steve to speak at your
event, call the following number:

866-445-5452

For more information, go to the following website:

www.stevegilliland.com

ACKNOWLEDGMENTS

I owe a unique expression of gratitude to my former acquaintances: those who once called me a friend but turned away from me when I needed them most. I recognize and thank them. While they may have got my goat temporarily, their actions allowed me to understand my inadequacies and made me a better person.

To every person who has intersected with my life and given me nuggets of wisdom and glimpses of truth, I am beholden.

To my sons, Stephen and Josh, who have stood by my side in the midst of my most challenging times, I am forever grateful. Your unconditional love and support was my inspiration to change my life and to make you proud to call me "Dad."

To my stepsons, Adam and Alex, who have provided me with a second chance to be a father, not just a parent, and who have taught me some valuable lessons: your strength during challenging times has been a great example of how to keep balanced in the midst of distress.

To my daughter-in-law, Amanda, who loves my son Stephen in spite of how much he acts like his father: we have grown together as a family and learned to love and accept each other for who we are. Thank you!

I very much appreciate being a grandfather. While I may not see my grandsons, Karter and Kiptyn, as often as I wish, I trust that I can leave a legacy that makes them proud to call me "Grandpa."

To my best friend, business partner, and soul mate, my wife, Diane, I cannot say anything that pays enough tribute to the incredible person she is. She is an exceptional wife, the world's greatest mother, and a friend who is always there for people, even when they are not there for her. Thank you for living my books!

To my friends, Jeff Dray (That's how you roll, dude!), Brian Hurst (Stay thirsty, my friend!), Bruce Montgomery (Well, it is!), Mike Cassel (Say it ain't so!), Lance Crumley (Really!), Bob Hewitt (Let's go racing!), Bob Crumley (See the end first!) and Skip Alberts (Okay, Coach!) who, regardless of my free spirit, have remained my friends: thank you for letting me be myself.

Finally, I owe special thanks to everyone who has helped me as a speaker and author for the past fifteen years—those who have never stopped believing in my message and me.

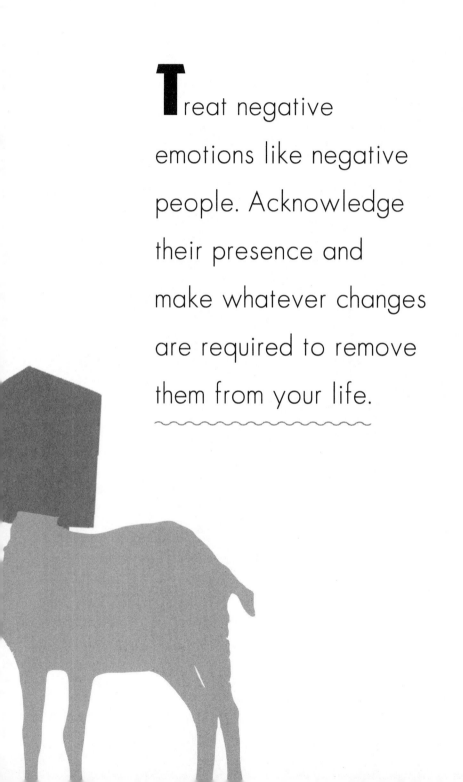

Treat negative emotions like negative people. Acknowledge their presence and make whatever changes are required to remove them from your life.

CONTENTS

INTRODUCTION

Whn you hear someone say, "That really *gets my goat*," they're not usually talking about an actual goat. Most often, they mean that they're very annoyed. The source of that annoyance could range from bad traffic to an unpleasant encounter. This useful idiom, apparently American in origin, springs like many figures of speech from shadowy beginnings, difficult to track down.

The expression first cropped up in common usage in the great boom years of early twentieth-century America when the country itself was a constant stew of self-invention and expansion, a rich time for linguistic coinage and the creation of slang. The influx of immigrants and non-native speakers of English only added to the mix, and many of the colorful phrases we take for granted today probably began their lives as corruptions of standard English, misunderstood and repurposed by these new Americans. It's been suggested in this context that the word "goat" is very likely a corruption of "goad."

Another possible source of its derivation is an old French phrase, *prendre la chèvre*, which translates literally to "to take the goat." Owning a goat was no small thing to a French peasant who might well depend on its milk and meat, so stealing somebody's goat in this context would mean robbing that peasant of income and food. Some etymologists have made note of the fact that goats were frequently used as companion animals for nervous racehorses, which might lead an underhanded competitor to steal a horse's favorite goat before a race in order to unsettle the horse and throw the race; thus, "get my goat."

Regardless of its origins, the expression "gets my goat" is something that resonates with all of us. Our daily lives intersect with a diverse group of people from different backgrounds who have unique opinions and personalities. The fast-paced, stress-filled schedules we maintain open the gate to allowing people and circumstances to get our goats. As you read this book, I will present ideas to help you herd your goats, lock your gates, identify people who may hunt your goats, retrain your goats, and follow nutritional (mental) advice on what to feed your goats.

I wrote *Hide Your Goat* to help you, the reader, maintain a positive and healthy attitude regardless of who you are, where you have been, and where you are heading. No one is immune to goat-getting; the infection can spread quickly, and those who discharge the poisonous toxin are masquerading as family members, friends, neighbors, coworkers, and a variety of other people. They believe that misery likes company; if they are unhappy, they think, why shouldn't they share the feeling? They are elusive, prefer not to march alone, and affect every institution of society. The venom they eject produces byproducts of bad attitudes, including resistance to change and personality conflicts. They hunt down upbeat people and, without regard, challenge the upbeat folks' outlook and question their positions on everything positive. They cost plenty in terms of productivity and morale, and they make life tough for everyone. They delight in getting your goat!

For the most part, these "goat hunters" are self-doubting, insincere, and, in a lot of cases, not even aware of the type of people they really are. Worse yet, they do not realize the unconstructive impact of their behavior or how other people truly perceive them. The people who accept the behavior of these other individuals are, more often than not, accepting a reflection of themselves. The challenge we all face is that, whether we like it or not, these people are family members, so-called friends, neighbors in close proximity, or coworkers who are not retiring anytime soon. So, how do you survive all this negativity? Hide your goat!

Just where do you hide your goat? It all depends on what you believe gets your goat, or, shall I say, pushes your buttons the wrong way. You are the person who chooses, every day, how you will respond to people and circumstances. You are the person who either has enough self-esteem to accept what life throws at you, or you are the person who feels a need to even the score. I wrote this book to help you rise above the dust of the daily battle that chokes and blinds so many of us when everything seems to be going wrong. Life's experiences will either make you bitter or better, stronger or weaker. The next time you are overwhelmed by misfortunes, hide your goat and let those events make you better and stronger.

Discover Your Goat

The Courage to Recognize Who You Are

M ost of us go through life without truly understanding ourselves. Some of us talk too much, give advice too quickly, get too angry, or fail to do what we have promised we will do. If we were to be honest with ourselves, we would admit that sometimes we might feel smug about a friend's plight, or value looks and money over integrity and kindness. Rarely do we allow ourselves to go much beyond these realizations. Understanding yourself is one of the most important tasks in hiding your goat. A great deal of pop psychology tells people to accentuate the positive and push aside the negative; yet, unfortunately, without recognizing the negative, people cannot fix it. For you, the reader, the first step to hiding your goat is to recognize and acknowledge your real self. It takes courage to be completely honest about who you are. So, *who are you?*

ARE YOU A WORRIER?

The most destructive habit you can have is worrying. I am now fifty-four years old, and I can honestly say I have worried about many troubling things that never happened. There are very few things in the mind that eat up as much energy as worrying does. Not worrying about anything is one of the most difficult things to do. People experience worry when things go wrong, but in relation to past happenings, it is idle merely to worry in terms of wishing that those things might have been otherwise. Meher Baba, Indian mystic and spiritual master, is famous for having said, "The frozen past is what it is, and no amount of worrying is going to make it other than what it has been." People also experience worry in relation to the future when they expect that future to be disagreeable in some way. In such a case, worry seeks to justify itself as a necessary part of the attempt to prepare for coping with an anticipated situation. Merely worrying can never help things.

"The frozen past is what it is, and no amount of worrying is going to make it other than what it has been."

MEHER BABA

Besides, many of the things that people anticipate through worry never happen; alternatively, if they do occur, they turn out to be much more acceptable than expected. Worry is the product of feverish imagination working under the stimulus of desires. It is living through sufferings that are mostly self-creations. As Meher Baba also aptly observed in his *Discourses*, worry does nobody any good, and in fact creates much unhappiness: "It is much worse than the mere dissipation of psychic energy, for it curtails the joy and fullness of life substantially."

As Corrie ten Boom explains, "Worrying is carrying tomorrow's load with today's strength—carrying two days at once. It is moving into tomorrow ahead of time. Worrying doesn't empty tomorrow of its sorrow; it empties today of its strength."

It is important to not lose today by worrying about tomorrow.

ARE YOU A GIVER?

The great joy in life is giving. It is extremely uncommon for people to give. Human nature motivates most people to guard and keep what they perceive to be theirs and theirs only. The more you give away, the more will come back to you. The more you help others, the more they will want to help you. As Glen Campbell's song, "Let Me Be a Little Kinder," entreats:

"Let me be a little kinder, Let me be a little blinder, To the faults about me. Let me praise a little more."

So, the question you must answer in complete honesty is this: Are you a giver?

> "The more you help others, the more
> they will want to help you."
> ## ZIG ZIGLAR

My advice has always been to earn as much as you can, save as much as you can, and, most importantly, give as much as you can. At age thirty-nine, when I was broke and life had given me all that I could bear, I made a promise to God that I would use whatever he would bless me with to bless others. The beautiful part of that is every time I bless another person, I always end up feeling more blessed. As the late, iconic, motivational speaker, Zig Ziglar, always said, "If you help enough people get what they want, you will always eventually get what you want."

Sometimes we let people get our goat because we are too focused on "making a living by what we get, instead of making a life by what we give," as Winston Churchill once said.

ARE YOU A FAULTFINDER?

Do you tend to find fault with someone or something all the time? Critical people cannot resist pointing out problems. Nothing is ever good enough. Faultfinders expect perfectionism in themselves and others. Unfortunately, finding fault or criticizing exposes the goat and almost always derails relationships and drives people away. Criticism does not get people to change, even if the criticism is valid. Worse yet, people will not trust the critic because they know, sooner or later, the critic too will fall prey to the criticism. People will become guarded. Eventually, all spontaneity will disappear, since they must carefully choose their words and watch their actions. Over time, they will not even want to be around that critical person.

Criticism does not get people to change, even if the criticism is valid.

Criticism, like swearing, is actually nothing more than a bad habit. Finding fault solves nothing; what's more, it contributes to anger and distrust in the world. No person likes to be criticized. A person who feels attacked will either retreat or attack and lash out in anger.

Many roads lead to negativity. People can become faultfinders if they live or work with negative people. Sometimes, in an individual family unit, one or both parents are critical. As a result, their child grows up learning to look at the world from a negative perspective.

If someone around you is pointing out mistakes, flaws, and injustices, it is easy to start focusing on mistakes, flaws, and injustices in life. If you know you are too critical, decide to change. Solve this problem by catching yourself in the act of being critical and reminding yourself of how it makes you feel when others criticize. Judging or criticizing another person says nothing about that person; it only reveals your need to be critical.

ARE YOU HUMBLE?

As my former secretary, Margaret, once told me, "Swallow your pride occasionally. It's not fattening!" Always trying to prove yourself to others places you on a slippery slope. Pointing out your own accomplishments takes an enormous amount of energy. Worse yet, the more you try to convince other people of your worth, the more they will avoid you and talk behind your back. As a well-known Chinese proverb states, "Arrogance invites ruin; humility receives benefits." Humility is such a weak and delicate thing that usually the people who think they have it do not. In order to be humble, you have to make the right estimates about yourself. The less you care about seeking approval, the more approval you seem to get.

"Too many people overvalue what they are not and undervalue what they are."

MALCOLM S. FORBES

In the industry of professional speaking, I have always tried to display a quiet inner confidence. For example, I had the honor to be asked to address my peers at our national conference. The person who introduced me said to the audience, "You are about to hear a speaker who has flown below the radar for years." I took that as the ultimate compliment.

Having humility does not mean you have to think less of yourself or have a low opinion of your talents; it purely means you should have independence from thinking about yourself at all. As Malcolm Forbes observed, "Too many people overvalue what they are not and undervalue what they are." Having humility is making an error and correcting it. A humble person is open to being corrected, whereas an arrogant person is clearly closed to it. Thomas Dubay, author of

Fire Within, says, "Proud people are supremely confident in their own opinions and insights. No one can reprimand them successfully, especially a peer. They know everything, and their arrogance does not afford them the capacity to see another view. They know—and that is the end of the matter." To paraphrase Thomas à Kempis, author of *The Imitation of Christ*, "If you want to know or learn anything to your advantage, then take delight in being unknown. Learning how to truly understand and humbly estimate oneself are the highest, most valuable lessons there are."

ARE YOU A GOSSIPER?

Nearly any time I hear someone start a sentence with the words "Someone said …," I can count on the rest of the sentence not being true. The best advice I was ever given was never to repeat anything to which I was not willing to sign my name. As a famous Jewish proverb suggests, "What you don't see with your eyes, don't witness with your mouth." Gossip hurts people, but most of us love to hear it anyway, and tabloids build financial empires on our appetites for other peoples' heartbreaks, divorces, and legal troubles. How can you differentiate between gossiping and simply sharing information about a third party with an interested mutual acquaintance? A simple test might be to ask yourself if you'd be so quick to share that story if the person it concerned was standing next to you. If not, you're probably gossiping, no matter how interesting that story might be (or how eager the person you're talking with is to hear it). Confident people don't feel the need to make themselves appear more interesting by tearing others down in their absence. If you're so hungry for approval and attention that you'll talk others down to get it, what does that say about you?

> While you may be able to control what you say, once you say it, it is open for interpretation and filtering by other people who may not express your exact intentions.

People who gossip are calling attention to themselves because they are seeking others' attention and approval. Sean Covey says, "Isn't it kind of silly to think that tearing someone else down actually builds you up?" It is easy for most folks to get caught up in day-to-day chitchat or to be curious about what is going on with other people. Comparing your life with the lives of others is natural. However, when you are bonding with people about shared friends and neighbors, it is easy for harmless information to turn into hurtful situations. While you may be able to control what you say, once you say it, it is open for interpretation and filtering by other people who may not express your exact intentions.

Gossip is like the proverbial loose cannon that once untethered wreaks havoc on all around it, on gossipee and gossiper alike. Do you really imagine that spreading scandal makes you look better, more interesting, or more "in the know"? Guess again. It's been said that in small towns, gossip travels at the speed of boredom. Leave the scandal mongering to the tabloids, and don't risk your friendships or your own reputation by reporting things better left unsaid.

ARE YOU A JEALOUS PERSON?

Do you constantly compare yourself with others, evaluate those others, and feel badly when someone else wins? Jealousy is a flaw most people have difficulty acknowledging in themselves. Holding back and not acknowledging someone else's achievements is a way jealousy raises its ugly head.

For example, I still remember the day a committee member informed me that I had been elected to the Speaker Hall of Fame. I called a fellow speaker, someone I had known for over fourteen years, to inform him of the honor. When I told him about the induction, he said, "I have been nominated several times and never got elected. Sounds as if you had the right committee voting." It was in that instant I realized something: When my friend got the attention of our peers in the speaking industry, our friendship was golden. You must look inside yourself for the reason you are jealous. The answer is there.

> "Envy hurts and does not give you what you are missing."
> **TEMMA EHREFELD, *OPEN GENTLY***

People compare themselves to others all the time, research suggests. When people decide they are inferior or lack some desirable trait or circumstance—be it beauty, intelligence, spare cash, or an apparently happy marriage—it is normal to feel hostile and focus on the perceived rival's faults and deficiencies. Sometimes jealousy arises from never feeling security from within. As Moshe Luzzatto, who has great insight on jealousy, explains, "Envy, too, is nothing but want of reason and foolishness, for the one who envies gains nothing for himself and deprives the one he envies of nothing. There are those who are so foolish that if they perceive their neighbor to possess a certain good, they brood, worry, and suffer to the point that their neighbor's good prevents them from enjoying their own."

The most destructive aspect of envy may be that it tends to hit us close to home, when those with whom we work or worse yet, in our own families, inspire us to envy. If your older brother is a gifted pitcher and a Little League All-Star when you're permanently stuck in the distant outfield, you can see only too clearly how much attention and admiration this earns him from others, probably starting with your parents. You may believe that if you'd had a better coach, you could have done as well, so the better he does, the worse you feel. The key to discarding envy is to remind yourself that it hurts nobody but you, and doesn't fill the need you have but only irritates it further.

ARE YOU AN ATTENTION SEEKER?

Similar to those who allow jealousy to control them are people who compete with others for attention. People who talk too much are competing for attention. As long as they keep talking, they have attention. What a person like that is really saying is, "Recognize me; pay attention to me!"

Interrupting is another competitive behavior that people adopt with the intention of diverting attention to themselves. Someone is telling a story, for instance, and the attention seeker interrupts and takes over. In a mode that is just as bad, some people compete with others by starting side conversations. In those situations, while one person is talking, the attention seeker starts a conversation with someone else. This is a maneuver used to take some attention away from the person who has the floor. Every time the attention seeker interrupts or starts a side conversation, he or she is conveying this message: "Pay attention to me. What I have to say is more important than what others have to say. I count more."

The emotionally mature person does not need to go hunting for attention.

People who seek to be the center of attention do not listen to others. When other people are talking, they allow their minds to wander and rarely ask questions or make comments. Another attention-getter is the emotionally immature person who has low levels of self-esteem and self-confidence; consequently, he or she feels insecure. A person who's saddled with this burden will expend an amazing amount of energy trying to counteract it, by creating situations in which he or she can shine as the center of attention. Some see this as a measure of maturity, or the lack of it, and the need for attention—almost any kind of attention—is inversely proportional to emotional maturity. Think of the little kid who can't stop hollering, "Look at me, Mom; look at me!" Just like that little kid, adults who can't stop begging for attention are signaling their own emotional immaturity.

This kind of attention-seeking behavior is only too common, despite the fact that it's ultimately a losing game. Being the center of everyone's attention may temporarily alleviate the insecure person's deep-seated sense of inadequacy, but because that feeling is really rooted in his low self-confidence and low self-esteem, attention is no permanent palliative for the correlated low levels of self-worth and self-love. The emotionally mature person finds those qualities in his or her daily life, through stable and satisfying interpersonal relationships. Daniel Goleman refers to this emotional maturity as emotional intelligence, or EQ; he believes that "EQ is a much better indicator of a person's character and value than intelligence quotient, or IQ."

ARE YOU CONTROLLING?

Why do people try to control others? For some people, hiding their goats is not possible because they do not think they are controlling. By not discovering their own goats, they expose those goats. The typical individual sees other people as controlling, which gets his or her goat. So, how controlling are you?

⇨ Do you talk too much?

⇨ Do you frequently offer unsolicited advice?

⇨ Do you have trouble apologizing?

⇨ Do you pout and refuse to talk when you get angry?

⇨ When you want something done, does it have to be done immediately?

⇨ Do you frequently run late?

⇨ Are you often accused of not listening?

⇨ Do you often jump in and finish another person's story?

⇨ Do you usually have the last word in an argument?

⇨ Do you insist on being the perfect host and waiting on everyone?

⇨ Do you finish other people's sentences?

A few years ago, someone close to me had the courage to point out how often I interrupted others and finished their sentences. Think about this for just a moment. I was hurrying people along and finishing their sentences, a behavior that annoyed and disrespected them. Not only was I not listening to what they were saying, I was also causing people not to want to interact with me. I was focused on controlling the conversation, hence getting people's goats and creating tension of which I was not even aware. If you desire good relationships with your colleagues, your spouse, your children, and your friends, you need to discover your controlling behavior and eliminate it.

DO YOU GET TOO ANGRY?

You know if you get too angry. You may not like to admit it, but you know if you have an anger problem. What you may not understand is what drives your anger, the consequences of getting too angry, or what you can do to change. Because our world is a pessimistic one, when an event happens, instead of putting a neutral or positive interpretation on it, you probably put a negative interpretation on it. By thinking negative thoughts, you actually create your own anger.

You can give meaning to an event in less than a second. Within a few seconds, you can have a number of negative thoughts. The people you surround yourself with play a significant role in how you interpret certain events. Negative people tend to form fellowships with negative people; hence, they increase the number of negative thoughts they are having and add fuel to the situation.

"Calmness of mind is one of the beautiful jewels of wisdom."

JAMES ALLEN, *SERENITY*

Another reason you get angry is the perception of a threat. Along with thinking negative thoughts when things do not go the way you expect, you may feel thrown off-balance, threatened, challenged, or not in control of the situation. Maybe the worst byproduct of getting too angry is you start name calling and exaggerating or become sanctimonious.

When presented with an event, any event, people make an interpretation. If we interpret the event negatively, we are likely to get angry. If we interpret the event more neutrally, we are not likely to feel angry. Some say that calmness of mind is one of the beautiful jewels of wisdom. It is the result of long, patient efforts in self-control.

To stay calm in situations, you must learn how to adapt to others. The more tranquil you become, the greater your success, influence, and power for good become as well. Ordinary people become extraordinary business people when they develop greater self-control. People will always feel more confident in dealing with someone whose deportment signals he or she is levelheaded and in control.

NO MORE ALIASES

Take an introspective journey to discover yourself. Who are you? The list of questions people must answer to determine identity could fill up an entire book. I once read, "A life not examined is like an unopened letter." If you don't know who you are, how can you possibly know who you want to be? Making a clear and honest self-assessment is an essential starting point for relationships, growth, and self-confidence. If you were dropped in unknown territory without a map, you'd have a tough time figuring out your location. Similarly, without a well-defined idea of who you already are, you can't hope to become the person you really want to be. Determining the identity you currently have is incredibly important to hiding your goat. Stop living your life under an alias. In order to improve you must first ascertain where you are, who you are, and then how you want to be. If you are not sure where you are, it is impossible to start making movements toward where you want to be.

> "Just as it is impossible to reach your destination when you do not know where you are, it is impossible to become the person you want to be when you are not clear on who you are."
> ## SCOTT H. YOUNG

If you do not know who you are, it is impossible to guard against the emotions and behaviors that expose your goat. Find the parts of yourself that you do not like and begin the process of changing them. Find the parts of yourself that you do like and accentuate them even more.

LOVE IT! MEAN IT!

What makes you different from your family, your friends, and the people with whom you associate on a regular basis? What do you like or dislike that maybe separates you from other people? Is there something deep inside you that brings you a certain amount of enjoyment, something that causes your family and friends to make it an issue and ultimately grab hold of your goat?

For instance, I love sports. That immediately causes some people to connect with me, and others to take the stance that I am a fixated sports fan who needs to dial it back a little. What would surprise most people is my reason for loving sports. I love sports because they are about loyalty, passion, and family. My family loves the Pittsburgh Steelers because Grandpa loved the Steelers, and nothing and no one is going to make us switch sides. A sport is not an escape from life; it is woven into the fabric of life. I also like sports because, as *Sports Illustrated*'s Rick Reilly once wrote, "there is no back door in which to walk. If you are Aaron Spelling's daughter and you want to act, you get to act. If you are a Trump, you get to build. In sports, nothing is handed to you."

This is not true any more Hollywood elite pay for kids to get into college sports

It is completely normal to be different as long as your behavior is not self-destructive.

My love of sports also encourages good, healthy detestation. If I am a Steelers fan, I am permitted to dislike someone for being a Dallas Cowboys fan. I can seethe about it and even poke fun at the Cowboys when I am speaking on stage. I also like sports because no two games are ever the same and it is new all the time. A Jeff

Foxworthy concert is the same 80 nights in a row. A Steelers-Ravens game is a new, epic event every time. If building model cars makes you different, so what? If you are a guy and love cats, adopt six of them. If you want to watch *Pretty Woman* 40 times and cry every time, watch it. If you enjoy watching birds, then watch them. It is completely normal to be different as long as your behavior is not self-destructive, since that kind of behavior can drive other people away.

THE DISCOVERY ICEBERG

Because the density of pure ice is about 920 kilograms and sea water's density is about 1025 kilograms, typically only one-ninth of the volume of an iceberg is above water. You can't tell much about the shape of the whole iceberg by what you see on the surface. This, of course, is the genesis of the phrase the *tip of the iceberg*, which describes a problem or challenge that's likely much bigger than is immediately apparent. Just like an iceberg, as an individual, you too have a great deal below the surface that only you can see. The portion people can see is the visible you, or the cliché level. It is the news, sports, and weather of your life; while it is sometimes trivial, most people communicate on this level. The part of you below the iceberg is the real you. This part is comprised of your unexamined life, secret mental life, purposes, priorities, goals, ambitions, motives, relation-ships, use of time, use of money, moral behavior, pride, fear, anger, problems, suffering, and discouragement. The challenge you face daily is the amount of insulation you have between the two levels. People tend to insulate themselves against themselves. They struggle to be honest with themselves and with other people who want to see what lies beneath the surface. The insulation is a double-edged sword. It can tear apart a relationship. All too often, people get beyond the insulation of a person, which can sometimes cause the former to look at the latter differently.

We tend to insulate ourselves against ourselves.

My experience has been that if you want to get below a person's surface, take a trip with him or her. In the span of twenty-four hours, you can tear down a great deal of insulation. If you do not want to spend the money on travel, invite the person over and have one too many cocktails. Chances are you will hear about that person's hurts, hopes, and fears, and you'll discover who that person really is. Before you go diving into the water, looking for the depth of another person's iceberg, acknowledge and discover what is below your surface. Like most folks, you probably tend to live your life wanting other people to believe you are the small portion they can see, which inevitably can be negative when the real you is revealed. Be honest with yourself, be honest with God, and be honest with your friends.

WHEN NO ONE IS LOOKING

The test of your character is what you would do if you knew no one would ever know. Who are you when no one is looking? Character is the stuff of which God knows you to be made. Your reputation is the stuff of which people think you consist.

Character isn't something that simply appears overnight; it develops over time. Many people believe that a person's character is set in childhood; whether or not that's entirely true, we can agree that it isn't subject to easy or fast changes. Each one of us has to be aware of who we are and what we want to be, in terms of our character. Others judge us, as we judge them, by the outward manifestations of our character; whether we present ourselves as strong or weak, bad or good. Do we manifest energy, drive, self-discipline, or are we vacillating and inconsistent? Just being strong isn't enough to guarantee we're also good. Plenty of criminal gang leaders, dictators, and other morally corrupt types have strong characters that make them attractive to weaker, less self-assured followers. Ideally, the world needs leaders who are both strong and good, who deserve trust and model good character to others.

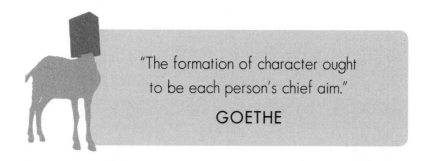

"The formation of character ought to be each person's chief aim."

GOETHE

As Indira Gandhi said, "There are two kinds of people in this world: those who work and those who take the credit. Try to be in the first group; there is less competition there." Numerous times I have said from the stage, "Watch your thoughts; they become words. Watch your words; they become actions. Watch your actions; they become habits. Watch your habits; they become character. Watch your character; it becomes your destiny." Character is the result of two things: mental attitude and the way people spend their time when no one else is looking.

BY OUR DEEDS

One night, a clergyman was walking to church when a thief pulled out a gun and demanded the clergyman's money or his life. When the clergyman reached in his pocket to hand over his wallet, the robber saw his clerical collar and said, "I see you are a priest. Never mind; you can go." The clergyman, surprised by the robber's unexpected act of goodness, offered him a candy bar. The robber said, "No, thank you. I don't eat candy during Lent." The man had given up candy as a supposed sacrifice for Lent, but his lifestyle of stealing showed his real character.

> When you habitually act a certain way, before long you will believe that it is not only normal but right, regardless of whether it is or not.

People demonstrate character every day by what they do, not just by what they say. Appearance and words can be deceiving; in contrast, behavior is the best measure of character. For some, facing who they really are can be very difficult. When a person habitually acts a certain way, before long he or she believes that it is not only normal but right, whether in fact it is or not. People who habitually do not tell the truth soon convince themselves that regardless of the falsehoods, their statements are actually true. Lying becomes a part of who they are and soon is their norm. Note to the reader: Until you are willing to embrace who you are, those who know you for who you are not will always get your goat.

JUST GROW UP

Think about how many times you have said, or heard, the following expression: "That person just needs to grow up." There are many things that bespeak maturity. Evaluate yourself according to the following maturity checklist. If you can put a checkmark beside nine of the ten, then you are almost there.

⇨ You accept that life is not fair and that, sometimes, bad things happen to good people.

⇨ You do not lose your temper: you do no screaming, name-calling, or pouting. You have learned to manage your anger.

⇨ You do not obsess about old hurts or disappointments. You have come to understand the power of forgiveness.

⇨ You do what you say you will.

⇨ You take others into account before making decisions.

⇨ You apologize when you make a mistake and you work hard not to repeat it.

⇨ You behave in a nonjealous way, despite the fact that sometimes you think jealous thoughts and have jealous feelings.

⇨ You freely give compliments and credit to others.

⇨ You work hard to keep the irritation out of your voice.

⇨ You understand that each belief you hold, each decision you make, and each behavior you present adds or subtracts from your dignity as a human being.

TAKE THE FIRST STEP

All of us have a propensity to improve our circumstances, but until we recognize who we are and become willing to improve ourselves, we will remain bound. Our goats will be vulnerable. Many people try to acquire wealth but are not willing to make great personal sacrifices. Their behavior is no different from that of the people who struggle financially and are extremely anxious about their surroundings, yet all the time they shirk their work and justify trying to deceive employers on the grounds of insufficient wages.

> Until you have the courage to recognize who you are and the willingness to develop areas of your life that need to be changed, someone or something will always get your goat.

We all want to live the "good life." So why do we undermine our progress toward that kind of life by hobbling ourselves with thoughts and desires that are so out of sync with our goal? Until you have the courage to recognize who you are and the willingness to develop areas of your life that need to be changed, someone or something will always get your goat. As philosopher James Allen put it, "Law, not confusion, is the dominating principle in the world; justice, not injustice, is the soul and substance of life; and righteousness, not corruption, is the molding and moving force in the spiritual realm of our world".

The initial step to hiding your goat is discovering yourself by seeking the things that are right. During that process, you will find that as you alter your thoughts toward things and other people, these other people will alter their thoughts or behaviors toward you. Before you can hide your goat, you have to discover that goat!

Herd Your Goat

The Strength to Accept
Where You Have Been

Far too many times in life we expect others to do what we have never done, follow us to where we have never been, and, without reason, believe in us even when our actions do not match our own beliefs. It becomes problematic when our actions, which create our outcomes, are determined by speculation, assumptions, misconceptions, and numerous other thought patterns that are not based on a situation's facts or reality. As children, we have two primary influences on our thinking: our parents and the time we spend around other people. Insecure adults have a tendency to create insecure children. Show me a mother who is a drama queen, and I will show you a child who grows up embracing the role of a victim.

41 |

The problem with herding goats is this: Where do you look for those goats? For some people, someone, or something, may have gotten their goats earlier in life, and they have never found those goats again. When these goats jump the fence and their owners have never been able to find them, the goat owners carry that with them for the rest of their lives. Instead of having closure and resolving their feelings, these people harbor resentment and become susceptible to having someone else or something else find another goat. The past is a powerful dictator of the future. Unless people can determine why they feel the way they do, they are destined always to allow certain things to get their goats.

THE CHOSEN CHILD

If I heard it once growing up, I heard it a thousand times. From the babysitter, my teachers, and even my father, I heard a consistent plea: "Why can't you be more like your brother?" Even when people did not come right out and say it, I knew they were thinking it. As a youngster, I needed to find and account for my goat, which had jumped the fence. Between the resentment I had for my brother and anger toward my father, it was a small miracle I did not run away from home. Well, I confess, I started to run away many times as a little boy, but I only lasted until I ran out of sandwiches. So, as a young child, I watched my father favor my older brother. As a young adult, I witnessed his approval of my brother and felt his disappointment in me. I did everything I could possibly do to win his approval. While Dad signed my brother's birthday cards "Love, Dad," he merely signed mine with his first name. By the time I celebrated my fortieth birthday, I was still seeking the approval of my father, family, and friends.

"It is not until much later, as the skin wrinkles and the heart weakens, that a child understands his or her parent."

MITCH ALBOM

In *The Five People You Meet in Heaven*, Mitch Albom says, "All parents damage their children. It cannot be helped. Youth, like pristine glass, absorbs the prints of its handlers. Some parents smudge, others crack, and a few shatter childhoods completely, fracturing them into jagged little pieces beyond repair. Parents rarely let go of their children, so children let go of them. These children move on, and some even move away. The moments that used to define them, such as a mother's approval or a father's nod, are covered by moments of their own accomplishments. It is not until much later, as the skin wrinkles and the heart weakens, that a child understands his or her parents." The final fingerprint on a child's glass (or youth) is when parents go silent when that child experiences his or her greatest accomplishments, silent when that individual builds a new home, silent after once being a significant part of the individual's life. Later in the book, Albom says, "Holding anger is a poison. It eats people from the inside. People think that anger is a weapon that attacks the people who have harmed them, but it is a curved blade. The harm people do in anger they do to themselves."

LABELING IS DISABLING

Have you ever watched a person you do not really know do something that bothers you so much it affects your attitude? Why does that person's clothing selection, earrings, hairstyle, or fingernail color get your goat? This topic reminds me of a gentleman who sat beside me on a flight from Amarillo to Dallas a few years ago. I could not help noticing the vast amount of tattoos he had on his arms, neck, and hands. What I noticed more than his tattoos, however, were the people across the aisle who stared at him and were clearly appalled by his appearance. I do not exaggerate when I say they were disgusted with his tattoos.

After I introduced myself to the man, he smiled, shook my hand, and told me his name. He asked if I lived in Amarillo or Dallas. When I told him I was from North Carolina, he said, "Great state. I got my MBA at Duke."

We talked the entire flight. When we landed, he said, "Thanks."

I said, "For what?"

"You are probably the first person I have sat beside in the last three months who has even acknowledged me without thinking I am a thug," he said.

Stereotypes attached to certain people
are not only unfair to them but are
also extremely unhealthy to the people
assigning those stereotypes.

This encounter reminded me of a goat that used to roam freely in my life: labeling. I discovered that labeling is disabling; the stereotypes attached to certain people are not only unfair to them but are also extremely unhealthy to the people assigning those stereotypes. Think about it: a passenger's appearance on a plane was able to get someone's goat without him even opening his mouth. Someone, somewhere, from the past of the person who stereotyped initiated a thought process that continued to roam loose within the margins of his or her being.

THE UNCOMMON, THE TYPICAL, AND THE SAD

I have always believed that if you can change the way you think, you will change your world forever. Looking at someone's Facebook page will easily determine how that person thinks. Uncommon people listen to, learn from, and edify other people. They will post pictures and information that is positive and intended to allow real friends and family to keep up with their important events and the growth of their children. Typical people talk about themselves. They will post information intended to inflate their egos and make themselves, their children, and their lives appear to be something they are really not. Sad and miserable people talk about other people. They will post negative things about other people.

> Looking at someone's Facebook page will easily determine how that person thinks.

Sad and miserable people will solicit responses to situations that should be handled privately and post quotes, underhandedly, to make a point. They thrive on the responses that make them feel better as people, which, unfortunately, does not make them better people. If anything, the majority of good-thinking people view them for who they really are: insecure, negative people filled with anger and unresolved issues. These folks have never had the courage to discover and admit who they are, and, even sadder, have never taken the time to herd their goats from the past and break the cycle of negative behavior that has been passed on to them from their families.

DIG DEEP

Recently, a former classmate invited me to join a group of old high-school acquaintances. He e-mailed me with the request: "A group of us is getting together to catch up. I saw you were going to be in Pittsburgh and wondered if you might want to join us." In his e-mail, he also reminisced a bit about our "glory days," which put a huge smile on my face. I was more than excited and let him know I would be delighted to join the group. In Pittsburgh, when I met up with the group at one of the local establishments, a few old acquaintances greeted me, and we joked about how gray each of us had gotten. No sooner had I begun to order a beverage when someone behind me tapped on my shoulder. I turned to see who was tapping and was met by a familiar woman's face that made me drift back in time. I remembered her cruel words of rejection that shamed me at a Friday-night postfootball game party. At that party, she had crushed my spirit and embarrassed me so much that I left within minutes, never to attend another game event. I remember that I thought somebody needed to teach her a lesson on how to treat people.

Liberate yourself by digging deep to let go of past bitterness.

Back in the present, I couldn't help but think of the Toby Keith song, "How Do You Like Me Now?" Although I felt as if I were reliving my adolescent pain, I mustered up my best fake smile and insincere words began coming out of my mouth. I actually said, "It is great to see you!" Before I could say anything else, a heartbreaking story of what had happened to her after high-school graduation began to pour out of her. As it did, the words my Bible-believing mother had referenced on more than one occasion, the "root of bitterness" (Hebrews 12:15), popped into my head. I realized that was what I was feeling. After all these years, I still had a deep root of bitterness hidden within me, twisting around and strangling my heart. As we talked and shared our life paths, I kept thinking about how blessed I was. Neither of us mentioned the long-ago incident.

I learned a lesson that evening, a lesson of forgiveness and of letting go of bitterness. As you herd your goats, liberate yourself by digging deep in order to let go of past bitterness.

CLEAN YOUR HOUSE

Every April, my mom would embark on her annual routine, doing what she referred to as her "spring cleaning." As a youngster who was required to help, I found the process arduous and yet liberating. Once you discover who you are, it is time to jump off the emotional roller coaster and accept where you have been. The process of cleaning your emotional house can be painful and is guaranteed to stir some emotions inside you. I recommend it to you without reservation.

Moreover, if you are ever going to hide your goat, it is something you must do.

THE CLOSETS

It is amazing what people keep in closets. I have found things for which I cannot even imagine a use. During one spring cleaning session, I found unmatched socks, a box marked "Wedding Pictures," and even two leisure suits. The box marked "Wedding Pictures" contained pictures of my sons' mother, from whom I was divorced years ago. The unmatched socks were a complete mystery, especially since I am a perfectionist. The leisure suits brought back some memories of seeing the movie *Grease* when it was first released in the midseventies, not to mention humorous mental images of me wearing those suits along with white platform shoes. If you do not know what a leisure suit is, you are too young. If you remember wearing one, you are my age. If you are still wearing them, seek help! During this cleaning, I also found stuff I did not remember having and stuff I was not even sure belonged to me.

> You will never get over the past without giving up some of it.

Most people's closets are cluttered with stuff they do not need. Likewise, people hold on to beliefs, prejudices, and hurts from a bygone past that are as outdated as polyester leisure suits. This can be very dangerous and detrimental to people's efforts to hide their goats.

If you keep holding on to stuff in your emotional closet that serves no purpose for the present or future, people and things will always get your goat. This emotional baggage may be made up of hurt feelings and past slights. It may be made up of judgments and conclusions you reached about someone or something.

One strategy for cleaning out your emotional closet is embracing the concept of forgiveness. You will never get over the past without giving up some of it. Carrying the past hurts, and pain is toxic to your emotional and physical health. It never allows you to move on to a new, better place. The more junk you stuff in a closet, emotional or otherwise, the more clutter you will have in your life and the more people around you will be affected. Once you clean out the junk in your closets, you will be able to feel the sense of accomplishment and clarity that comes from having some room in your life. You will be able breath and stretch out a bit.

THE WINDOWS

People often tell the story of a boy who found a penny at the age of six. From that day forward, he set a goal to begin looking for money every time he was outside walking. By the time he turned eighteen, he had found 263 pennies, 28 nickels, 17 dimes, 21 quarters, 2 half-dollars, and 9 dollars. His total net gain was $20.98. In the old days, this amount of money would have gone a lot further than it does today. Regardless, what he did not realize was what he lost. For, you see, he lost the following: 21,900 sunsets; 67 rainbows; and over 2 million smiles. Like the boy in the story, having the wrong focus can cause you to be up some days and down others. If you focus continually on the negative things from your past, you will never see the beautiful things of today.

Take, for example, the people who have experienced a bad relationship in the past, one in which they have been deceived, cheated, and totally disrespected. By focusing all their energy and attention on their previous pain, they are never able to see beyond the "dirty window" that inhibits their view of new people who are honest and respectful.

> If you are a person who cannot seem
> to get over the past, take at look at
> what you need in the present.

There's a reason our minds continually work over the events of the past, and usually I find that reason has to do with what's happening right now. Is there an unmet need you're feeling that reminds you of some other time in your life when your needs went unmet? Is something in your current life making you feel that familiar old tug of fear, or stab of pain? Talk about it with someone who really knows you, and whom you trust. Just hashing it out and saying what you're feeling can make it all much clearer. That frees you to begin to figure out what need is unmet in your life today, and how you can go about fulfilling it. Your preoccupation with the past is your mind's way of helping you to see the present more clearly, and the sooner you identify what's really troubling you, the more quickly and decisively you can deal with it.

For better or worse, until someone builds a working time machine, the past has passed and can't be changed. The best we can do is to acknowledge it, do our best with the present moment, and move on.

THE GAME ROOM

The television room, the game room, the "great room," or whatever you call the place where you go when you want to expend virtually no mental effort, may be the hardest room to clean in your house. The game room is a metaphor for habits. Every time you perform an activity, it gets easier and easier to do; after a certain point, almost no intellectual exertion will be involved. The opposite of this is also true: whenever you refrain from an activity, it becomes increasingly more difficult to perform, until you have virtually no desire to perform that same activity.

Everything that appears in life first originates from thoughts. If a habit is in your life, you know the parents of that habit were, and continue to be, your thoughts. One single negative thought can kick-start a habit, leading to a multitude of additional negative thoughts, which bring about actions and finally harden into habits. Your habits become your character, and your character dictates how you go through life. Think about it; this big, dirty, rolling snowball of undesirable consequences got its start from just one negative thought! Take action; block that negative thought, and resist the others that follow it. That is the only way to insure your success in blocking the adoption of any negative habits.

> Your habits make up your character, and
> your character dictates your life.

It's easier to avoid taking on a bad habit than it is to get rid of one that has taken hold. There's no straight, smooth path or one-size-fits-all solution, but the first step is recognizing and acknowledging that bad habit. Brainstorm strategies to counteract that habit. Some habits come attached to certain activities or locales; that bakery across the street from your office, for instance, might have lured you into indulging on a too-regular basis in something you know isn't good for you. Take another route to work, or keep something healthier in your desk to snack on. If you're trying to break a smoking habit, stay away from places and situations that make you want to smoke. If you're dealing with a drinking or substance-abuse issue, avoid the people with whom you drink or use drugs. Picture yourself resisting temptation; work out coping strategies ahead of need, and you'll find it easier to actually resist when the occasion presents itself. Keep trying different strategies until you discover what works for you.

THE DINING ROOM

If you give nonsensical instructions to people or computers, those instructions will produce nonsensical results: hence the phrase *garbage in, garbage out.* Just as you clean house thoroughly, it is crucial to clean your mind thoroughly, especially as the concepts you are going through relate to your past and where you have been. As you will learn in Chapter Four, what you feed your goat is very important in determining what it will take to hide your goat.

People produce tons of trash annually, and they do so not just in the form of candy wrappers tossed into the trash bins outside on the sidewalks, the newspapers taken to the recycle bins, or the half-eaten food thrown down garbage disposals. Whether it is through reality television shows, late-night infomercials, or bad romance novels, people take in a great deal of trash annually. Where does the mental trash go from there? Eventually, it is recycled in the form of negative thoughts, which proceed along habitual pathways until they become permanent negative attitudes.

THE ATTIC

As a child, I always enjoyed visiting my Aunt Shirley. However, once there, I was afraid to go into my cousin's bedroom, which was where the access door to the attic was located. My cousin would tell me stories that sounded real. Sometimes he would say he could hear screams and moans coming from behind the closed door at night.

Just like my fear of the attic at my aunt's house, we all have fears that need to be eliminated. Fears live in people's heads and hearts, and they hate being kicked out. Denying a fear only makes it stronger. Acknowledge it and then investigate it. Explore it. Find out where it came from, whether it's fear of doctors, dating, or even like my son Josh, a fear of flying. Find out why you are afraid.

As you herd your goat, you have to accept where you have been and determine what makes you fearful. That fear cannot hurt you any more. Accept your fear for what it was, not what it is, and release it.

NEVER PLAY TO NOT LOSE

Until you reach a point at which you stop overthinking things and start overcoming the fear of what might happen on the other side, you will never live your life to the fullest. People tend to overanalyze certain facets of life to the point at which they are not really living. As the popular sports expression goes, people are "playing not to lose the game." The translation of this expression is simple. Some players or people approach everything so cautiously that they never fully expe-

53 |

rience what they could. They spend more time and energy worrying about what might be, only to wonder later what might have been.

A REALITY CHECK

There are three possible ways to perceive reality: How you see things, how others see things, and how things really are. Based on your past experiences and conditioning, everything that has happened to you in your entire life has led you to believe that this is the way the world works. The influence of your parents, spiritual leaders, teachers, and neighbors has had a powerful impact on how you view the world. When a person you know acts in a manner contrary to your own view, the action either opens up the gate for you to become negative or allows you to gain a perspective you never realized, which may cause you to grow.

> How you see something, or how someone else sees it, is not as important as how things really are ...

...for you see (pun intended), other people's past experiences and conditioning, which is different from yours, has led them to believe the way they do. Again, you may offer them a perspective that allows them to grow, or you may create a disagreement that pits your goats against each other. Ironically, how you see something or how someone else sees it is not as important as how things really are. If you try to achieve this perspective whenever possible, you will have the best chance of hiding your goat in every situation.

MAKE A LEGAL U-TURN

Whenever I drive her somewhere, my wife asks about my sense of direction. After I make a wrong turn, the GPS will affirm her suspicion and say, "When possible, make a legal U-turn." These days, millions of drivers recognize that phrase, or a similar one, as a sign they have gone off track or missed a turn. The GPS device not only recognizes when a driver is off course; it also immediately begins plotting a new path to get the vehicle back on track.

Sometimes, people veer off track early in life, and, unfortunately, they never get back on track. At times, it can be unintentional; at others, people veer off course because they think they know best; alternatively, people drift away slowly, failing to notice they are moving further and further from where they need to be. More often than not, an internal alarm sounds and triggers people's consciences, begging them to face the goats from the past. In that case, they may ignore the warning, but they do so to their detriment.

FULL SPEED AHEAD

Financial expert Warren Buffett, now one of the richest people in the world, was rejected by the Harvard Business School at age nineteen. After a failed admissions interview, he recalls a "feeling of dread," along with concerns over his father's reaction to the news. In retrospect, Buffett says, "[Everything] in my life ... that I thought was a crushing event at the time has turned out for the better." Even as I am writing this section of the book, Warren Buffett is in the midst of purchasing H. J. Heinz in a deal worth $28 billion. Rejection, though undeniably painful, does not have to hold people back from accomplishing what they believe they can do. When rejection becomes a hindrance, reach down and go full speed ahead. Sometimes, it is a rejection that provides you the strength to accept where you have been.

A MIRROR REFLECTION

James Moses, a judge at the 2013 Westminster Kennel Club Dog Show, once said, "If your dog licks you in the face every day, how can you be objective?" Just as some dog owners struggle to accept the scoring their dogs get at dog shows, most people are equally challenged to look in the mirror and accept their flaws, not just see those flaws. It is virtually impossible to hide your goat until you discover it, understand it, and finally herd it. People's views of the world, and especially of the people who inhabit that world, are, in most cases, mirror reflections of who they truly are. Ever wonder why some people get so angry at other people's behavior, even to the point of ridicule? Could it be that the things they don't like in other people are the goats they have not herded?

> When you are not happy with something in your own life, it is usually magnified twice over when you view it in someone else's world.

Additionally, when a person close to you provides you with make-up to cover one of your warts, metaphorically speaking, they reinforce behavior that can breed negative responses to various situations. When you are not happy with something in your own life, it is usually magnified twice over when you view it in someone else's world. Controlling people struggle with controlling people. Rude people become even ruder to compensate for a feeling of violation, regardless of the circumstances or, more importantly, who is right or wrong. There are many reasons people fail to face their goats. Embarrassment, fear of rejection, and bitterness are a few. However, people's fear of change is a central part of their acceptance of things they know in their hearts to be troubling.

ACCEPT WHERE YOU HAVE BEEN

Herding your goats is critical to hiding them. You cannot hide them until you find them. People will always be vulnerable to other folks or circumstances getting their goats. However, once they herd their goats, they can begin to build a stronger fence around those goats.

How does this apply to you? You have to be honest with yourself and resolve the issues in your own life before you can expect to keep your goat fenced. It's been well and truly observed that the mastery of life is the mastery of self. Unfortunately for many people, they never master themselves, which leaves their goats outside the fence, waiting to be taken.

Unresolved feelings produce detrimental behaviors, which in turn cause more nonconstructive situations.

Make a list of what and who gets your goat. Most importantly, include questions of how and why. What is it about you that affixes to the negativity of each situation? Once you determine your contributions to the situations on your list, figure out what you need to do in order to change the way you think about the situations. For example, my unresolved feelings about my father led me down a path of thinking that produced detrimental behaviors, which in turn caused more unconstructive situations. Years ago, instead of just being who I really was, I was doing almost anything to be accepted by people, especially my father. As I did, when you seek the approval of others, you act in ways that are all about the people you are trying to impress.

> The saddest part of someone getting your goat is when you fail to take away a powerful message and a transformational lesson from that experience.

You must allow yourself to acknowledge the emotions that are attached to your past and own them. You have to feel your feelings and free yourself to move into a more focused state. While some of these challenges may have been painful, you are required to own them nonetheless. Do not blame a relationship with someone, or lack thereof, on everything and everyone but yourself. You must take responsibility for your role in everything, knowing full well it is not just you and that you have absolutely no control over other people. That is tough for some people to swallow because they so desperately want to blame and change other people. However, you cannot change people; you can only change yourself. The saddest part of someone getting your goat is when you fail to take away a powerful message and a transformational lesson from that experience. Sometimes, that message is readily available, and you can move on after you have processed and digested it. However, in some cases these lessons will come much later in life. Wait for such a lesson because it is out there. When you uncover it, your attitude will change, and so will your life.

THREE

Teach Your Goat

The Wisdom to Discern
Where You Are Heading

Have you seen the movie *The Bucket List*? It's about an unlikely friendship that develops between blue-collar mechanic Carter Chambers (Morgan Freeman) and billionaire hospital magnate Edward Cole (Jack Nicholson) who meet at a point when each of them has just been diagnosed with terminal cancer. Carter begins keeping a "bucket list" of all the things he meant to do in life but never got around to, a list his new friend Edward finds and encourages him to try and accomplish, goal by goal.

What would you do if you knew you were destined to "kick the bucket" in the foreseeable future? The film got a lot of people

59 |

thinking about just that. Since the movie's release, numerous people have adapted its terminology and will say things like, "That's on my bucket list," referring to something they want to do before dying. There are even websites devoted entirely to the subject where people can log in and catalog all the stuff they want to accomplish before they expire. Writing a book, getting a tattoo, seeing the northern lights, learning to play the guitar, learning Japanese, skydiving, and swimming with dolphins are just a few of the items on people's bucket lists.

> While making a list of wishes allows people to dream about possibilities, it sometimes causes them to overlook basic needs necessary to live more fulfilled lives.

What if people focused on a list that was not a bucket list, but rather a "fill the glass" list that would center on achieving personal satisfaction while living? People expose their goats to possible incarceration when their center of attention is on their wants, fantasies, and wishes instead of their needs. You see, a *need* is a must for you to be your best. Sometimes, it can help to identify needs by thinking about times when you are angry, upset, or doing something of which you are not particularly proud (for example, procrastinating). What is it that causes you to have certain feelings or to do certain things? Look deep and you are likely to find a need.

To hide your goat, you must teach it new tricks. You must identify your needs, why they are important to you, and what are you doing to meet them. While making a wish list allows people to dream about possibilities, writing such lists sometimes causes people to overlook basic needs necessary to live more fulfilled lives. When a glass is not completely full, a person will tend to focus on it being half-empty rather than half-full. However, that person forgets that his or her point of view is based on whether he or she is pouring or drinking. People are inclined to approach life in a very similar way. People know there are things they need to do (pouring), but they focus more on the wants (drinking) because it is seemingly more gratifying.

> Until you recognize your negative needs and change your behavior, you will always be predisposed to people and circumstances that can get your goat.

If people, time after time, ignore areas of their lives they need to change, they are left defenseless against the feelings that coincide with their unmet needs and will see the glass as half-empty. It is important to remember that people all have contradictory (pouring or drinking) needs. For some, the need is to be accepted, cared for, acknowledged, and comfortable. For others, it is to be free, be in control, and be right.

Regardless of what your needs list looks like, it is imperative to make a list in order to understand what sometimes causes your goat to get loose and even attack others. While there is nothing wrong with wanting to be accepted, you must determine why that is so important to you. Is it because you want to be respected or popular? Do you need to be comfortable because it allows you to indulge or serve? Do you need power to be noticed or influence other people in a positive way? People can all recognize the need to change, but somehow they trick themselves into believing that things can remain the same and actually get better. That is not going to happen.

Effectively, an individual's ability to hide a goat requires an understanding of where he or she wants to go. Until people recognize their negative needs (old goats) and change their behavior (teach the goats new tricks), they will always be predisposed to folks and circumstances that can get their goats.

TEACH YOUR GOAT TO BE HAPPY, NOT RIGHT

Several years ago, I met an elderly couple in Seattle, Washington, while enjoying the breakfast buffet at the hotel at which we were both staying. I couldn't help but notice how attentive and servant-hearted the gentleman was toward his wife. Since our tables were in close proximity, I commented to him on his caring ways and then asked him a couple of questions. My first question concerned the length of their marriage. The man boldly answered, "Sixty-five wonderful years."

My follow-up question was, "What is the key to staying married for sixty-five years?"

His response was one for the ages. He proclaimed, "The key to being married for any length of time is to determine early in the marriage that you would rather be happy than right." Many times, being right does not make people happy, but being happy makes everything right. When people are happy, it is harder for other people to get their goats.

"Needing to be right, or needing someone else to be wrong, encourages others to become defensive and puts pressure on those with the original need to keep defending."

RICHARD CARLSON, *LET OTHERS BE "RIGHT" MOST OF THE TIME*

Being right and defending positions takes an enormous amount of mental energy; often, it alienates individuals from the people in their lives. Richard Carlson also noted that "Needing to be right, or needing someone else to be wrong, encourages others to become defensive and puts pressure on those with the original need to keep defending." My wife has an aunt who believes it is somehow her responsibility to show others how their positions, statements, and points of view are incorrect. In doing so, she believes the person she is correcting is going to appreciate it, or at least learn something. Wrong! It is not that it is never appropriate to be right, but usually such an action comes from the ego suppressing the soul and ruining an otherwise peaceful encounter. If this sounds like something you do, why not teach your goat to participate in and witness others people's happiness? That is far more rewarding than participating in a battle of egos.

TEACH YOUR GOAT TO STOP TELLING IT LIKE IT IS

When I hear a person proclaim, "Whether you like what they say or not, at least you know where they stand," I know that where they stand is in a position to hurt other people via their self-righteous proclamation. Ultimately, it just makes the speaker feel better, not the person to whom they're speaking their "truth." Remember, a closed mouth gathers no feet, and you will never regret your silence. People who criticize others receive guidance from their own perspective, which is almost always void of the total truth.

Good things usually happen to people who talk positively in negative situations.

Your mouth is a tool that can be a powerful force of hope and encouragement. Your words can either build up or tear down another person. There is tremendous power in the tongue. Good things usually happen to people who talk positively in negative situations. Teaching an old goat this trick is not easy. Training yourself to speak words that are uplifting, that bless others, and that create opportunity is a tough task, particularly if you have the need to be heard, gossip, or make a point. Consider that when you tell something like it is, you are really showing people more of who you are than of whatever it is you're telling them.

TEACH YOUR GOAT THE ART
OF BEING, NOT DOING

When you are physically run down, short on sleep, and bothered by low energy levels, you tend to be more irritated, critical, defensive, and negative. It is hard for you to get along with others and harder for them to coexist with you. According to T. D. Jakes, "Fatigue is the silent cancer of judgment and emotions. It steals your energy and discernment. When you are fatigued, even simple problems seem insurmountable."

So, when you are tired, go to bed. Turn off the television, shut down the computer, and silence your phone. Fatigue can cause you to make permanent decisions based on the stress of temporary circumstances. Instead, take the necessary time to rest and renew, so you have the energy to hide your goat.

Children today are not taught the art of relaxing or just being; they are constantly doing.

Much of the anxiety and inner struggle people endure stems from their busy, overactive minds; they need something with which to entertain themselves. Today's children are being raised in a culture that is built on the philosophy, "What's next?" Children are not taught the art of relaxing or just being; they are constantly doing. Today's technology does not permit people to relax and disconnect. Being relaxed involves training yourself to respond differently to the dramas of life and always reminding yourself that you have a choice in how you respond to life. With practice, making the right choices will translate into sustaining a more relaxed state of mind, which will permit you to head in the right direction.

TEACH YOUR GOAT NOT TO LISTEN TO SKEPTICS

A Western Union executive memo written in 1876 stated, "The telephone has too many shortcomings to be seriously considered as a means of communication. The device is inherently of no value to us."

My favorite memo of all time comes from a recording company executive who wrote, in 1962, "Don't like their sound ... guitar music is on the way out." Of course, after this man rejected the Beatles, they went on to become the most successful musical group in history. Do not let other people blow up your dreams. You will always encounter opposition from ordinary people. High achievers struggle against overwhelming obstacles in the face of sharp criticism, but they have the heart to pursue when others quit. When people are hunting your goat armed with criticism, skepticism, ridicule, and disbelief, you will have to reach deep down in your bag of tricks and not permit them to make you doubt yourself. Heading in a new direction begins with you.

Not knowing what a change will bring
can tempt you to stay with what you
know, even if it is not what you want.

To do away with doubting yourself, program your brain to think positive thoughts and send messages that ultimately will assist you in taking charge of your life. By doing this, you will eradicate the *I can't* and *I shouldn't* vocabulary from your thought process. Phrases such as *I can't* and *I shouldn't* render you powerless. When you are fearful of the unknown, you are less than enthusiastic about a new direction or change. Not knowing what the change will bring can tempt you to stay with what you know, even if it is not what you want.

Think about one goal you want to accomplish; then, assess why you are not accomplishing it. It may surprise you to find that *I can't* has been so prevalent in your thinking that *I choose to* and *I can* have never been a part of your mental vocabulary. Do not limit yourself just because people will not accept the fact that you can do something else. The only thing worse than not teaching your goat new tricks is allowing a skeptic to make you doubt yourself. Today is the day to say, "I choose to and I can!"

TEACH YOUR GOAT TO BE CONTENT

When I was growing up, my stepfather worked in a steel mill in western Pennsylvania. We lived in a neighborhood where virtually every household was dependent on a blue-collar job. Most families had one car, which was parked in a gravel driveway. We had burn cans in the backyard and a septic tank in the side yard. Our water supply was from our well. While we did not reside in a row house on a city street, our housing was considered modest, with only a few neighbors residing in brick homes nearby.

Two miles away was a neighborhood where the homes were all built of brick and the square footage of each was double of any home in our neighborhood. My friend Bill lived in this neighborhood. I remember vividly how excited I was whenever he invited me over. I would marvel at his family's kitchen and the carpeted stairs up to his bedroom on the second floor. That's right, they had two levels and a finished basement. Are you kidding me? Bill was one of the few kids in my class whose parents both worked: his dad was a salesman and his mother, a nurse.

The thing I remember most was Bill's motorbike and all his toys. He seemed to have everything. I do not know how many times I said to my mom, "You should see Bill's motorbike."

She would reply, "Your success in this lifetime will not be based on what you have, but rather on who you are. Your stepfather works hard to put a roof over your head and food on the table. You may not have a motorbike or a bunch of toys, but you have two parents who love you." Of course, back then, no offense, I would have preferred a little less loving and a few more toys. Now, today, I am glad I had the loving over the toys.

> The competitive spirit in people drives them to compare, to complain, and to covet.

Contentment is hard to attain. How do you learn this? You learn to be content one step at a time until you are satisfied even in uncomfortable environments. You must learn to accept whatever comes your way and receive, with thanks, whatever you are given. Contentment is not natural for any of us. Teach your goat to be content. As Benjamin Franklin once said, "Content makes poor men rich; discontent makes rich men poor." Perhaps most people's idea of a contented person is the one individual, if any, who enjoys the scenery along a detour.

People today live in a world in which competitive spirit drives them to compare, to complain, and to covet. I am not suggesting that people back in the '50s and '60s did not compete, compare, complain, or covet, but I do believe there are a great deal more goats loose today than there were back then. We are already on the fifth edition of the iPhone. Correct me if I am wrong, but I believe people all want the latest version of what everyone else has. Sometimes people's goats run loose and dictate behaviors within them that are detrimental to themselves and others. You do not need a new car every three years, another upgrade on your phone, or five wine openers. What you need is a car that is paid off; this will reduce your stress and permit you to be content. The key is to teach your goat the difference between what you want and what you need.

TEACH YOUR GOAT TO BE REALISTIC

Why are good relationships so hard to maintain? Why is there no such thing as a perfect marriage? Why would someone live his or her entire life with a few friends but never have one to call his or her best friend? Could it be that people's expectations are based on something other than what they truly want? Are people chasing the end of the rainbow to find the pot of gold, while deep in their hearts they know it does not exist? If relationships were easy, all people would have good ones. You have to teach your goat to be realistic.

> Excessive demands without clearly
> defined expectations create
> outcomes that are not realistic.

Take a person who is married and his or her spouse is not meeting his or her expectations. Try to think about what it would have been like when the two were first dating and what they truly expected from their relationship. When did their expectations change? Take another example: a friend who enters a friendship without any expectations. As time goes by, those expectations form, and when those expectations are not being met, the friend finds a way to escape.

Using wisdom to discern where you are heading in life can be a complex process due to the numerous relational issues you may have placed in jeopardy because of your own shortcomings. Add in the issues involving other people that you cannot control, and you have a perfect storm for hurt feelings, resentment, and, in some instances, damage that cannot be repaired. More often than not, when your expectations are beyond realistic attainment, you set yourself up for justifiable anger. Excessive demands without clearly defined expectations create outcomes that are not realistic. Clarity and communication are essential for good relationships. Spell out your expectations and confirm that others share this understanding. Determining if your expectations are realistic can be a great help in taking care of yourself.

TEACH YOUR GOAT TO LEARN THE HARD WAY

Allowing your children to make their own decisions and suffer through some difficult times will offer them the opportunity to become self-reliant, rather than parent reliant. How many times are cheerleaders chosen based on popularity, rather than an exact set of criteria? How many times are coaches' children allocated to play in the most popular positions in Little League because of their parents' involvement? Too often, parents intervene to ensure their children's happiness, happiness that was not necessarily deserved or earned. When people lack trust in their children's desire to be competent, they often are fulfilling their own childhood losses. Instead of allowing their children to head in their own directions, these parents choose those directions for their children based on previous experiences. This is an enormous lesson to teach your goat.

It is more harmful to overparent than to underparent.

Is it any wonder why people bring up so many young adults who lack the resolve to stick to anything that throws an obstacle in their path? Young people want to make their fortunes quickly and without struggle. I am always amazed when someone says to me, "It must be nice. I would give everything to be in your position." When someone says that, I simply respond by explaining that I did. I am now convinced it is more harmful to overparent than to underparent.

The more people rescue children at an early age, the more people set those children up later in life to have the littlest of things get their goats. My mother was right when she said, "You'll just have to learn the hard way." Adversity has a lot of valuable lessons to teach.

TEACH YOUR GOAT NOT TO SAY IT, TYPE IT, TWEET IT, OR POST IT

It is one thing to lose your cool **consciously** when you elicit an intended response from a person; it is another thing to lose your cool because your emotions unknowingly cause you to lose self-control. You will end up creating a dent in your own image. You also will be unable to express your points coherently, and you might end up saying something you regret later. In contrast, you will never regret your silence. When you are emotional, usually you wind up saying the wrong things. If it happens during a phone conversation or a meeting, deal with it professionally, with your anger parked aside. No matter how angry you are, get ahold of the anger and do yourself a big favor: don't say it, type it, tweet it, or post it. Before you send an e-mail, let the text sit in your head first and get back to it at a different time. Vent later, when you are with your friends, but do not vent to the person in question in a way that will later come back to bite you. Once an e-mail is sent, it cannot be unwritten. How many people have posted something on Facebook or tweeted something on Twitter that they later regret? How many apologies, lawsuits, damaged careers, and broken relationships have resulted from people's inabilities to teach their goats to stay calm in various situations? While you are at work, conduct yourself professionally. Doing so is telling of your ability to handle *stress*, as well. If you cannot conduct yourself appropriately, you are not going to earn the respect of others. If your mouth is closed, you cannot stick your foot in it.

TEACH YOUR GOAT NOT TO TAKE
THINGS PERSONALLY

When people face rude folks, it is easy for them to put the blame on themselves. They think there is something wrong with themselves, or perhaps there was some unappealing quality about them that triggered such reactions in others. Even though they might react in jest, or get all riled up, the folks they are really upset with are themselves.

It is always great to have that level of introspection, because that is the key to growth. There may be something about you that made people react a certain way to you. However, that does not mean there is something wrong with you. Those people chose to take issue with you because that is simply their nature, their construct as people; their beliefs, values, conditioning, and past experiences made them act that way toward you. **Their rude behavior is really more about** their story and **personal issues than it is about you.** So do not self-depreciate. Their rudeness is not entirely because of you.

TEACH YOUR GOAT TO FOCUS
ON WHAT YOU HAVE

If people threw their problems in a pile and saw everyone else's, they would grab their own right back. If you are facing a difficult situation right now, you are not alone. All humans tend to complain about the way that their lives are going. No one is perfect. When people take a step back and truly analyze their lives, they see that they have it so much better than many people around the world. It is estimated that 1.6 billion people do not have enough food to eat. That is a very large number of people who go hungry every day. If you can feed yourself and have clothes to wear, you are better off than many people. If you have a warm bed at night, you are well ahead of many others. Accept the reality of your current situation and circumstances, and try to improve your life. Unless you are in a truly bad situation, your life is not as bad as you might think. Many famous people and rich people are miserable and unhappy, even though they are financially secure.

> The next time you sit down and think your life is bad, remember all you have to be grateful for.

If you have the eyes to read this and good health of which to be proud, you are very fortunate. Yes, money is important because it allows people to support themselves. There are other things people have in their lives that they tend to overlook. The next time you sit down and think your life is bad, remember all you have to be grateful for. All of us have experienced a time when we have been frustrated by the direction in which our lives have gone. Many people have wondered why they are not getting hired. It is easy, sometimes, to feel life is bad and going nowhere. It can get better if you focus on all the good things you currently have.

TEACH YOUR GOAT TO STOP OBSESSING ABOUT BEING LIKED

Do you put a lot of energy into second-guessing how others see you? Are your decisions often made on that basis? Do you have an unquenchable need to hear people praise you? Do you look to others to define for you who you ought to be? Are you buying into the misunderstanding that someone else knows you better than you do? How does it affect you when you realize someone doesn't like you?

You can have a theater full of people applauding, but if you see that one person sitting on his hands, does it rob you of all your joy and make you even more eager to please that single holdout? Now hear this: What other people think of you is none of your business.

Fixating on how others see you or how to make them like you is just spinning your wheels.

People pleasers are made, not born, usually because of hurtful interactions with others in which they were made to feel inadequate or unlovable. One too many bumps like that, and people can very quickly become wholly committed to remaking themselves to please others rather than being the people they really are.

Our egos drive us to seek to be liked, approved of, and validated. It is natural to want approval, to want to feel lovable. But the downside risk is that constantly striving to conform to others' notions of what we should be not only exhausts us but also moves us ever further from the truth of who we are. Don't let your need to have the approval of others make you hide your genuine self. Do know that if you're dwelling on how others see you, it's not really about them but about you; specifically, it's about your ego.

Think of what you could accomplish if you took all that wasted energy you expend trying to win over others and put it into something really meaningful, sharing your true self, your gifts, and your talents. You've lost touch with these aspects of your true self because you have been so invested in playing it safe.

TEACH YOUR GOAT TO LET GO

If you are holding on to hurt, pain, or rejection, cut it loose. If you're pouring your love into a leaky vessel—someone who can't use it much less return it—cut it loose. If someone has gotten the better of you and it's making you crazy, cut it loose. Maybe you're imaging how one day you'll bring down the one who's hurt you; cut that idea loose. If you know you're in a no-win situation with dependence, whether it's on a person or a substance, cut it loose. If you are holding on to a job that no longer meets your needs or abilities, cut it loose. If you're dragging around a no-win attitude and it's weighing you down like a cannon ball, cut it loose. If you sit in judgment on others because you fear how they might judge you, cut it loose. If you're hobbled by constantly seeking approval from family, friends, or coworkers that isn't freely given, cut it loose.

Pessimism, cynicism, and distrust are byproducts of trying to fit in.

People, for the most part, seek to be liked and accepted. While they may say one thing, their actions do not match their so-called beliefs. As I wrote several years ago in my book *Enjoy the Ride*, this behavior would explain why some people spend money they do not have to purchase things they do not need in order to impress people they do not even like. Growing up, you were probably challenged with fitting in; years later, you are still seeking approval from your family members, friends, neighbors, and coworkers. Pessimism, cynicism, and distrust are byproducts of trying to fit in. Surviving the negativity that surrounds you is rooted in cutting loose everything that drags you down, holds you back, and impedes you in thinking positively. Until you are able to be confident in your own thinking, you will forever hold on to people and circumstances that keep you from heading in the right direction.

TEACH YOUR GOAT TO CHANGE AND GROW

As Pastor Joel Osteen says in his book *Become a Better You,* "You can never change what you tolerate. As long as you accept it and accommodate it, you're going to stay right where you are." If you do not change (that is, start teaching your goat), you will not grow. If you do not grow, people can get your goat without even trying. If you do not have the power to change yourself, do not expect your surroundings to change.

When Albert Einstein said, "The definition of insanity is doing the same thing over and over and expecting different results," he was referring to people who were trying to fill a bucket with holes. Forget your bucket list of before-you-die goals and start on a needs list of things you need to change while you are living. The irony is that the typical individual entangles a bucket list with a needs list and thinks of the result as his or her goals. To hide your goat, you have to teach your goat. Teaching your goat is about acquiring the wisdom to differentiate between what you want and what you need, to get you where you are heading.

FOUR

Feed Your Goat

The Knowledge to Acquire
What It Takes to Get There

Most people are conscious of the negative consequences that can arise from eating unhealthy foods. However, the majority of people pay little or no attention to the effects of what they are currently feeding their minds. As I explained earlier, the idiom *garbage in, garbage out* refers to the fact that giving nonsensical instructions to people or computers will produce nonsensical results. Equally true is the statement that your mind will give back exactly what you put into it. Unhealthy foods may satisfy your hunger, but they may also break your body down in the long run. Psychologists call it the negativity bias; our minds perceive negative information as being more distinctive and more novel than positive information. The fact that it has more novelty means that it will be remembered more frequently and be easier to recall. However, over time this negativity will become a natural part of you, which will make it harder for you to be positive.

Never spend time with a thought you do not want to experience.

It is important to take responsibility for what you are feeding your mind. You can either feed it mental "protein" or mental "candy." When you do not choose to feed your mind what is useful and beneficial, you leave yourself defenseless against people who are hunting your goat. Be selective about what goes into your mind. Never spend time with a thought you do not want to experience. You must have an appetite for the thoughts, language, and beliefs that will allow you to live and experience the life you desire. It is crucial that you reprogram your mind with positive input. The most significant decision that you can make on a day-to-day basis is your choice of attitude, which becomes either your best friend or worst enemy. What you feed your goat on a daily basis determines your attitude toward yourself, other people, and how you live life.

CHANGE YOUR MORNING THE NIGHT BEFORE

Suppose you go to bed late. The house is a mess and the dishes are piled in the sink. You are way behind on laundry, and you do not have food for breakfast or lunch the next day. You wake up with your goat being frazzled, stressed, and behind. As an alternative to trying to get up too early and pack in an extreme quantity of things in the morning, **focus on changing your before-bed routine first.** You might find that this is the thing that will transform your morning much more effectively than getting up earlier. You need quiet time in the morning. Quiet morning time is a very important part of a day. It is the time when you can anchor all of your thoughts and prepare for the new day or unwind from the previous one. Take the time to read something inspirational or positive. Spending just a few minutes this way might make a big difference in your daily life.

Start the day right with a morning routine that feeds your mind.

You owe it to yourself to wake up and relax. The definition of *oxymoron* is a phrase in which two words of contradictory meaning are used together for special effect (e.g., "wake up and relax"). As Sydney Harris explains, "The time to relax is when you don't have time for it." When you start your day by hitting the snooze button ten times and then rushing to get ready for work, you miss feeding your goat and deprive yourself of the energy essential to having a balanced day.

Approached correctly, the morning tends to have a quieter, more contemplative feel. Take advantage of it by following poet William Blake's advice to divide up your day: "Think in the morning and act in the afternoon." Start the day right with a morning routine that feeds your mind. If your job is more about cranking things out than managing and contemplating, you can use the mornings, when you are not on a tight deadline, to think over problems, consider future challenges, and give your tasks more mindful attention. The best part of waking up in the morning is waking up to an organized day. Count your blessings and take a little time to relax.

START YOUR MENTAL METABOLISM

The next time you stop in Starbucks for breakfast, you may want to take into consideration the fact that what you get there will not hold you over until lunch. Even if you think it will, eating there will not help your body gain the energy it needs to burn the calories it should. Worse yet, such a meal does not get your metabolism revved up and burning as much body fat as possible. The morning is an important time to kick your body's fat-burning process into gear; by doing so, you can lose more weight throughout the day.

People have all heard that breakfast is considered the most important meal of the day, and for good reason. Food is fuel and energy for the body. Without it, people spend the day stumbling around in a fog, fighting off headaches and bad moods. Breakfast is, as it sounds, breaking the fast that your body has undergone since the night before. Consumption of breakfast increases your metabolic rate and kickstarts your body into gear, telling it what to expect for the rest of the day. Without breakfast, your body does not process your next meal as quickly and, therefore, tries to hold on to those nutrients. Those who skip breakfast have a tendency to consume more food than usual and have a higher tendency to snack on high-calorie foods, which can lead to a number of problems when it comes to weight control.

If a 30-second commercial can sell you a product, what do you think the first 30 minutes of your day can sell you?

Your mental metabolism works the same way as physical metabolism. Mental metabolism has been described as the process of sorting, processing, digesting, and eliminating the byproducts of thought. This is an absolutely integral component of transformation, expansion, and growth. Just as your body needs to eliminate toxins, your mind requires the elimination of contaminant thinking and byproducts of mental metabolism. How you start your day is a tremendous factor in determining the remainder of your day. Just as a quick latte will not give you the energy necessary to burn calories, the wrong mental food will not give you lasting mental energy. Turning on the news and reading the newspaper will fill up your mind, but at what cost? If a 30-second commercial can sell you a product, what do you think the first 30 minutes of your day can sell you? I am not saying a coffee at Starbucks the first thing in the morning is not good, but a steady diet of coffee by itself, without proper nutrition, is very bad for your health. Similarly, a steady diet of negative information used to start your day without anything positive will leave your goat standing by the fence ready to jump.

Feed your mind with information and ideas that are uplifting, those that make you feel happier and more confident about yourself and your world.

Feed your goat the mental protein and fiber it needs by reading something inspirational and uplifting every morning. Start your day without e-mail, Facebook, or Twitter. Resist the temptation to read the newspaper or watch the news. Instead, spend a few minutes reading a good book or periodical. Feed your mind with information and ideas that are uplifting—those that make you feel happier and more confident about yourself and your world. Choose the most important task on your radar over checking your e-mail. Whatever arrived in your inbox overnight likely is not as imperative as the most important thing you need to work on in the morning. You would not know it, though, the way most people handle mornings. If you want to look back on your morning with a greater sense of satisfaction at having made it productive, take control of it by choosing one task and making it your priority for one uninterrupted hour. Don't even check your email! It may seem sacrilegious, but what you accomplish will surprise you and defrag your mental storage. So, start your day by feeding your goat something that will start your mental metabolism.

TAKE YOUR DAILY VITAMINS

When was the last time you supplemented your daily routine with activities that could enrich your outlook? Everyone needs diversity in life. Unfortunately, many people reach a point of burnout that affects them mentally, physically, and emotionally. This burnout can turn a positive attitude into a negative. When you are not feeding your goat the right stuff, you begin to look at things in more negative terms; you begin to feel trapped and helpless, and you begin to be more fatigued than normal. Here are some "vitamin supplements" or activities you can use to feed your goat:

⇨ Read a book for enjoyment.

⇨ Attend a play or concert.

⇨ Invite friends over for the evening.

⇨ Play with your children.

⇨ Take a two-week vacation.

⇨ Exercise for 10 minutes every day.

⇨ Take a drive with no destination in mind.

⇨ Take a class or lesson for enjoyment.

⇨ Participate in a hobby.

⇨ Attend a social function.

TAKE A BIG GULP AND SWALLOW YOUR PRIDE

No one in history has ever choked to death by swallowing his or her pride.

Every day people are subject to a diet of minor irritations, criticism, sarcasm, and deception. When you are faced with these annoyances, you may be tempted to retaliate because your self-esteem is involved. The key is to swallow your pride. Whenever you lose sight of your goals, you lose all perspective and deviate from your objectives. If a fight breaks out in the middle of a basketball game in which you are playing, you should not get involved in the skirmish. While you may believe your dignity is at stake, your goal is to win the game and not to hand out bloody noses. If you get involved in a fight and get thrown out of the game, you have been beaten. Remember, your original objective was to win the game.

> When faced with challenges,
> true character is exposed.

Pride is a self-focused emotion. Sometimes, you will feel awkward in your own skin. As with most things, everything to which you struggle to adjust will pass. Accept your missteps and learn from your mistakes. How you grow during this period will have a dramatic impact on your future. When faced with challenges, true character is exposed. The best way to hide your goat is to take a big gulp and swallow your pride. Feed your goat more "soul" food and stay away from "ego" food.

IGNORE THE FOOD CRITICS

While sitting in a barber's chair, a salesman mentioned he was excited about an upcoming trip to Rome. The barber, an Italian, was a very critical man. "You'll be disappointed," he said to the salesman. "Rome is very overrated. The service in the hotels is horrible. The airlines have all kinds of trouble. You'd better stay home."

The salesman insisted he was going to Rome to close a big business deal. He hoped to see the pope while he was there. The barber shook his head in disgust. "You'll be disappointed trying to do business in Italy. Nobody buys there and you'll never get to see the pope, since he only sees important people."

Two months later, the salesman reappeared in the barbershop.

"How was your trip?" the barber asked.

"It was wonderful," said the salesman. "The flight was smooth, the service in the hotel was perfect, I made a big sale, and I got to see the pope."

The barber was astonished. "What happened when you saw the pope?"

The salesman said, "I knelt down and kissed his ring. He patted me on the head and said, 'My son, who gave you such a lousy haircut?'"

The greatest way to even the score is to ignore.

> People tend to criticize most loudly in the area in which they have the deepest emotional need.

People are all criticized occasionally. Ours has become a very critical society. People pay other people to criticize music, art, politics, athletes, movies, and food. People even criticize speakers and authors, and that they do for free. I am convinced that some people, if they had been present at the feeding of the five thousand, would have criticized Jesus for not providing lemon for the fish or enough butter for the bread.

Yet there is such a thing as constructive criticism. Sometimes, a loved one may criticize you to direct you toward excellence. If somebody shares a loving word of constructive criticism, you need to appreciate and pay attention to it.

Most of the time, however, criticism is not constructive. It is not meant to build people up, but to tear them down. Usually, people do not hear of such criticism directly, it is not factual, and it serves no positive purpose. People tend to criticize most loudly in the area or areas in which they have the deepest emotional need. Even the world's most renowned chefs are criticized. Regardless of who you are, or how good a person you are, you will always encounter critics. The best practice is not to take into account the negativity or the critic who is trying to create it.

QUESTION YOUR PERCEPTIONS

If you ever watched the television comedy Seinfeld, you know whom I am referring to when I remind you of George Costanza. George was a paranoid person who lacked self-confidence and was constantly misperceiving situations. Misperceptions can ruin relationships, reduce productivity, and rob you of self-confidence. People's reactions to events are based on core beliefs they have developed about the world and themselves. People develop these underlying beliefs based on past experiences, including childhood experiences. Their underlying beliefs can cause them to interpret behaviors incorrectly and possibly cause problems.

If you assume a perception is true, eventually it will become a belief.

As a case in point, suppose you are at a charity event attended by numerous people. You make eye contact with and greet an acquaintance as she is walking right past you. She seems to be looking directly at you, but she does not respond. In fact, she does not even nod her head in your direction. What is your perception of that event? Do you instantly surmise that something is wrong and she is mad at you? If you assume a perception is true, eventually it will become a belief. When you believe a person who failed to acknowledge you does not like you, your brain will look for evidence to support that belief and allow you to use it to explain all future interactions. One wrongly perceived 10-second party encounter could completely change the nature of your relationship with that person. Instead of succumbing to your perception, approach the person later, at the same event, and ask if she saw and heard you earlier. There could be many valid explanations for her behavior, such as daydreaming, not wearing her contact lenses, or having just received a text message from her babysitter that has her frantic about something that just happened at home with her children.

THE SIDE EFFECTS OF ADDITIVES
AND PRESERVATIVES

The majority of foods in the fast-food industry contain some kind of preservatives so that their quality and flavor is maintained and bacteria and yeasts do not spoil them. While these additives are useful in extending the shelf life of the foods, the effects they have on those who consume them may not be so salubrious. It's been suggested by research that they may be the root cause of a whole spectrum of health problems, ranging from allergies, asthma, and headaches to ADD and hyperactivity.

Be careful of feeding your goat in a social and intellectual environment that encourages false intimacy and feigned friendships.

Social media is the societal version of fast food. Social media has taken a hug and a smile and packaged it into a "Happy Meal," pun intended. I am not suggesting that you close your profile on Facebook, but I am warning you about the dangers of social media. Be careful of feeding your goat in a social and intellectual environment that encourages false intimacy and feigned friendships. Facebook can lure you into fake relationships and into participating in a self-serving community. Just like additives are used to inhibit the growth of bacteria, molds, and yeasts in food, social media is intended to enhance, not inhibit, a relationship. Too much of either can produce lingering, negative side effects.

While I may live outside the digital bubble, my warning about feeding your goat too much social media is for awareness, not denunciation. Be honest with yourself. The majority of people on Facebook promote themselves in a certain way to cause other people to think of them in a certain way. People on Facebook are constantly twisting the truth to offer their so-called online friends the best parts of their lives. Their goal is to have their friends view them as cool, funny, or great at parenting, or as the kind of people they may not be and are struggling to become. Even online pictures are used as a form of boasting and promotion. People who use social media continually invent ways to make themselves look better and keep up with everyone else. They seek the approval of others, and when they do not get it, their goats are exposed. Boasting and self-promotion are foods that allow people to find and get your goat.

Just like developing bad eating habits, feeding yourself too much social media is a dangerous precedent that can invite possible unwanted outcomes. An illusion that can have devastating results, such as the need to share every aspect of life, can lead to constant status updates that not only make a person look needy, but also border on privacy issues. As author Nick Westergaard points out in a piece in *The Gazette*, "Personal information a person would normally share during an intimate conversation is instead shared with hundreds, maybe thousands, of followers. While people can see the reactions online, no one knows how an update affected the poster's personal life at home."

Reaching out through cyberspace, rather than picking up the phone or meeting a friend for lunch, can be polarizing.

My son Alex has battled an elbow injury that has necessitated eight surgeries. He needed one surgery to control a serious infection that had spread throughout his arm. His doctors had to call in specialists, and it was a very traumatic time for all of us. What started as another outpatient surgical procedure turned into a seven-day hospital stay. News of Alex's setback spread through his high school, his workplace, our church, and our neighborhood. Unsurprisingly, people's use of Facebook accelerated the news instantly. Alex's Facebook account exploded with people posting comments on his wall.

Naturally, my wife and I visited Alex in the hospital, and she stayed with him every day and night until his release. By the end of his hospital stay, only one "friend" had visited or even talked with him via telephone. Most chose to merely text or post. Ironically, the instrument that helped keep Alex connected with over four hundred of his friends became their tool of choice for "visiting" him in the hospital. His smiles were reduced to LOLs and people expressed feelings of compassion by typed words only. Reaching out through cyberspace, rather than picking up the phone or meeting a friend for lunch, can be polarizing. If you put something out on Facebook, you may get some response from your hundreds of (added and preserved) friends, but it may turn out to feel rather hollow. That is not the foundation for an intimate connection; it is more of a delusion.

BEWARE OF THE HARMFUL INGREDIENTS

Statistics show that the bulk of the American family food dollar goes to purchasing processed foods, most of which are pumped up with additives and stripped of their essential nutrients. Many dieticians have suggested people should discover which common ingredients in the foods they eat pose the greatest risks to their health. For many people, their goats are at risk of being found due to experiences (to extend the metaphor, ingredients) as a result of a conflict with family at some time or another. A person's personality traits, attitudes, and behaviors are the result of experiences at work and at home. More notably, people struggle to avoid these harmful experiences, or ingredients, because they remind them of their natural way of life: being raised in a dysfunctional home. "Dysfunctional" is a popular and probably overworked buzzword in popular psychology today, so let's settle on a meaningful definition. The Texas State at San Marcos Counseling Center's brochure, *Dysfunctional Family Patterns*, defines it as follows: "A dysfunctional family can be characterized by extreme rigidity in family rules, little or no communication, high levels of tension and/or arguing, extended periods of silence, blame and avoidance as primary coping mechanisms and an overall message of 'don't feel, don't talk, don't trust.'" For other people, it is more of a lifetime struggle involving much confusion and emotional pain.

For some of us, understanding the harmful ingredients we were fed early in life and making changes to avoid them later is a big challenge. Change is something that we human beings naturally resist and distrust, and that may be even more of an issue for the adult child of a dysfunctional family. But the hard fact is that it's up to the individual to make the change; it's not something that can be accomplished by committee. If you're waiting around for others to change, why are you? They may well be waiting for you!

Here are five common harmful ingredients that must be acknowledged and removed from your diet:

⇨ *Abandonment:* Fear of being left behind plagues many people who were raised in dysfunctional homes. They feel left out, unimportant, or simply forgotten. Common sense tells us that it's no reflection on the inherent worth of a child who's been abandoned, but, rather, the fault of the adult whose responsibility it was to care for the child. That's easy to say, but hard to accept for those who bear the scars of childhood abandonment well into adulthood. The pain and deep-seated mistrust abandonment engenders can last a lifetime. The injured must come to acknowledge and understand the extent of their injuries before those scars can heal. If they do not, they can create lasting disruption throughout adult life. Even working life can be affected, as it's been noted that any kind of change—layoffs, mergers, even a positive change like a promotion—can be perceived by the adult child of a dysfunctional family as yet another abandonment.

⇨ *Control:* People from dysfunctional homes often see control as a major issue in their lives. This is typically because they have either been dominated by overly strict parents or allowed to run wild with no parental supervision. Control freaks have to run every relationship, from home to work. Compromising or negotiating is nearly impossible for them; it's their way or the highway. This overwhelming need to control everything in their environment springs from fear, although the unfortunate control freaks aren't likely to understand or acknowledge that. The fears that drive them—the fear of failure, abandonment, or loss—are too overwhelming to allow them to unbend and let others take the wheel.

⇨ *Boundaries:* This involves the inability to say no and set reasonable limits. People who grow up in dysfunctional homes may not be able to differentiate among their needs and those of other people and other situations. People with low self-esteem are dependent on others' approval and recognition; they are, therefore, fearful of rejection by or conflict with others. It's been noted that people with low self-esteem tend to have problematic relationships, probably because they're unwilling or unable to establish healthy boundaries with others. On the job, this inability to say no and set limits translates into workaholic behavior.

⇨ *Denial:* Denying or avoiding reality is a learned behavior for those from dysfunctional families. It functions in that unhappy atmosphere as a way for dysfunctional family members to lull themselves into a false sense that everything is okay, when in fact it's not. Denial lets them live in their illusions, using their fears, hopes, unmet needs, and insecurities to hold them prisoner there. When you are in denial, you refuse to admit the truth or reality of something unpleasant. In a work environment, denial results in running from the truth or internalizing issues rather than confronting them.

⇨ *Drama:* Overstimulating events, such as confrontations, crises, emergencies, and calamities, become part of a way of life in a dysfunctional family. One way some emotionally immature and needy folks find to survive is to make themselves the center of attention. Their low self-esteem and poor self-confidence is boosted when they're busy creating these emotional dramas, in which they can star. It's pretty clear that the hunger for this kind of attention is inversely proportional to emotional maturity. Therefore, anyone indulging in attention-seeking behaviors is really just showing off how emotionally immature he or she is.

Attention-seeking behavior is surprisingly common. Parents dressing three-year-olds in Lucky Brand jeans, Ralph Lauren sweaters, and Nike tennis shoes, or pushing their children around in Coach strollers, are seeking attention. As you read earlier, Facebook is a great platform for people who need to be noticed to alleviate their feelings of insecurity and inadequacy. However, the relief is temporary since the underlying problem remains unaddressed: low self-confidence, low self-esteem, and consequent low levels of self-worth and self-love. Some people seek out that adrenaline (or sugar) rush, which gives them the feeling of security and adequacy.

GET ABOVE THE DRAMA

One reason the wrong perception of a situation can ruin relationships is because people gather friends and acquaintances and share their perceptions (not facts) of situations they have experienced. As they did in the Old West, people round up a posse and hunt down the explanations they believe best fit their situations. People spend hours, days, and several conversations trying to find the answers so they can officially, and metaphorically, hang them.

Have you ever analyzed the conversations you have with your friends? Do you spend more time talking about something or someone? I believe that great people talk about ideas, good people talk about good deeds, average people talk about tragic events, and uninformed people talk about people.

> Though there may be some facts hidden in an agenda, perceptions are not usually based on the truth; they are emotional energy drainers.

Your perceptions can run wild, and take you into the tall grasses of imagining frightful scenarios that may or may not have any genuine connection with a relationship situation, or event. From an emotional standpoint, some mistaken perceptions can appear to be rooted firmly in reality. Though there may be some facts lurking in there, they're usually few and far between. The sad fact is that they're an emotional energy drain. The only way to get a clear perspective is to detach yourself, and get above the fray. From that vantage point, you'll have a much better view of the situation, your part in it, and what others may have contributed. It's easier by far to take in the construction of a drama when you're watching it like an audience member, rather than acting it out with the other "performers".

LAUGHTER IS THE BEST MEDICINE

As a professional speaker, I have always believed that if someone is laughing, he or she is listening. If someone is listening, he or she is learning. It's been said that humor is infectious, and I can testify from my own observations that a good laugh is more catching than a cold. Shared laughter is a uniquely human experience that binds us together, lifts our spirits, and supports our physical health. It's been proven in fact that humor and laughter strengthen your immune system, boost your energy, diminish pain, and lessen the damaging effects of stress. Best of all, this medicine comes free and has no harmful side effects. Nothing works faster than a good laugh to lighten stress or defuse a tense situation. Even the simple physical act of smiling by itself has been shown by recent research to lift your mood. Laughter brings us into balance, puts things in proper perspective, and reminds us not to take ourselves or anything else too seriously.

People with a good sense of humor who laugh daily are more likely to have healthier hearts.

Want to improve your immune system? Laugh more. Want to feel better physically? Laugh more. Want to feel better about life generally, and share that good feeling with those around you? Laugh often and out loud. Research has shown that the health benefits of laughter are far-ranging, possibly even linked to better blood sugar levels for diabetics and to the production of disease-fighting antibodies. Think I'm exaggerating laughter's beneficial effects? People with a good sense of humor who laugh daily are actually more likely to have healthier hearts. A study by the University of Maryland found that people with heart disease laughed or smiled 40 percent less in general. The researchers concluded that laughing is likely to protect the heart.

Humor starts with ourselves; it's part of acknowledging our own silliness, our need to cut loose and get back in touch with that giggling child within we too often lose touch with when we become adults. Lighten up; start by poking some fun at yourself. Cultivate an appreciation for the ridiculous, and share it with those around you. Humor is like a muscle; the more you use it, the better it works and the more easily you can access its strength. If you have a sense of humor, make sure it gets a good workout.

YOU'RE RESPONSIBLE FOR YOU

An old Cherokee is teaching his grandson about life. "A fight is going on inside me," he said to the boy. "It is a terrible fight and it is between two wolves. One is evil; he is anger, envy, sorrow, regret, greed, arrogance, self-pity, guilt, resentment, inferiority, lies, false pride, superiority, and ego. The other is good; he is joy, peace, love, hope, serenity, humility, kindness, benevolence, empathy, generosity, truth, compassion, and faith. The same fight is going on inside you, and inside every other person, too." The grandson thought about it for a minute and then asked his grandfather, "Which wolf will win?" The old Cherokee simply replied, "The one we feed."

Feeding your goat the right diet will help you achieve your goals by staying positive and not exposing your goat. If you don't feed your goat the right stuff you will allow negativity to grow and aggravate you and the people around you. People don't like to admit they are negative, but there is no hiding it, and just as important, it will not go away without addressing it. Remember, you're not responsible for changing or "fixing" the whole family's diet. You're responsible and in control of taking care of yourself and making the changes you want. Changing your goat's eating habits is difficult and takes time. Be patient with yourself.

FIVE

Gate Your Goat

The Awareness to Exclude Who Is Stopping You

ave you ever been wronged? Have there been times when you haven't gotten everything you deserved? Have you spent your time and energy on what should have been or have you focused on what can be? Even when truth and justice are on your side, you may never be able to right your wrongs. A major diversion from hiding your goat is when you allow destructive emotions regarding people to consume your energy and make you negative. As you look backward, trying to right your wrongs, have you become resentful, angry, hateful and bitter? Instead of worrying about someone making it right, refocus yourself so you can move forward. Every mistake, broken promise and slip-up, can develop a paralyzing grip. Stop wasting priceless hours envisioning revenge toward an uncaring person. Resentment is about other people who seldom give thought to their offense. Remove all the resentment, jealousies, unforgiving feelings, and self-centeredness and just let go. It is imperative that we gate our goats to ensure they never stray beyond the boundaries of where someone or something can get them. While closing the gate may seem simple, it is a process that involves several components to ensure no one from the outside can get in, and what is on the inside cannot be lost or taken.

If you care what people think, you will always be their prisoner.

A principal reason we need to hide our goat is because of the different people who calculatingly and unintentionally hunt our goat. This list of people can include family members, coworkers, bosses, subordinates, neighbors, acquaintances, children, and utter strangers we encounter on a daily basis. We open the gate for our goat to "get out" when we focus too much energy on what other people think, how they act, and what they say. If you grant people permission to hurt you, they will. They can't hurt you unless you let them. If you care about what people think, you will always be their prisoner. If you are bothered by their actions, you will always be uptight. You can't change people!

ACCEPT REALITY

Have you ever encountered a person whose personality seems to poison whatever water they're swimming in? No matter what the situation, these folks can make it that much worse, more emotionally fraught, and more painful to endure. They're called toxic, and with good reason. You can point out to one of these folks that they're poison, but don't expect them to believe you. Whether it's some underlying personality disorder or some other factor that makes them the negativity magnets they are, hardly matters. What does matter is how you deal with them, if and when you must. The big thing is to preserve your own sanity. Impossible people are out there; you can't fix them, and you can't always avoid them. If you feel as though the person you're dealing with is toxic, you're probably right. Don't waste your energy trying to make him or her see the light. It won't work and will likely just antagonize him or her further. Sometimes— most often, in fact—the only wise course with these people is to stop arguing and step back. You'll never bring them around, and continually running into a brick wall is liable to give you a headache without altering the wall one bit.

OPPOSITES DRAW YOU IN

Winston Churchill and Lady Astor had a running feud. They were constantly attacking one another. Once, following a crude remark by Churchill, Lady Astor sneered, "Winston, if you were my husband, I'd put poison in your tea." "If you were my wife, I would drink it," he answered. We have all heard that opposites attract. While interesting and infatuating initially, over the long haul the attributes that are foreign to us become irritants as time progresses. Spouses and friends who share similar viewpoints, religious or spiritual ideas, personality traits, and ethnic and economic backgrounds have a far better chance of long-term successful relationships than those who are quite opposite. Spouses and friends must determine how to spend time and money, and those who produce children, must share similar ideas on how to parent in order to provide a peaceful environment for success. When you have a daughter-in-law who believes that she is the only female to ever birth a child, it can create some tense moments with the in-laws when you don't share the same ideas about parenting. Throw in her dysfunctional family who share her parenting skills and you will have some interesting holidays with your grandchildren.

> Spouses and friends must determine
> how to spend time and money.

A few years ago I asked a friend of mine if he could fix a go-kart for me. He said he would be more than happy to help, and when the task was completed, sent me an invoice for his labor at a cost of $40 per hour. Let's just say the total bill was more than I paid for the go-kart. The incident almost severed our friendship. However, when we finally got over the episode, we both agreed that, in the future, we would establish expectations when it came to money. A spouse or friend who differs enough to expand your life experiences and thinking is beneficial as long as the core values and internal moral compass are similar for both of you.

BREAKING UP WITH YOUR FRIENDS

Sometimes friendships become unhealthy and need to end. How do you know? Too many times they are getting your goat by using you for selfish ulterior purposes, or their natural personality ends up irritating or hurting you constantly. While "breaking up with a friend" is difficult, it is necessary if you are going to put yourself and your needs first. Life should not be mind-numbing and wearisome. When you prolong relationships with people who see their world through tainted glasses, you are at risk of being imprisoned by their views and not your own.

Unlike family relationships, friendships are strictly optional. You're certainly not required to continue them if they've clearly gone past their expiry date. There are a whole host of reasons that might be the case, from clear deal breakers such as abuse of trust to the simple fact that you've grown apart and no longer have the same kind of interests. Go with your gut, and avoid polling other mutual friends about what you should do. They may have a vested interest in one outcome or the other, or feel compelled to choose sides.

> No matter what you will say or do, it can never make the situation right, so you all too often overlook it and continue the circle of the irrational and wondrous entanglement referred to as "friendship."

Don't let a sense of obligation make you spend more time with people than you really want to. It's not doing them any favors, and your resentment is liable to show. Some people demand more attention and devotion than you want to give; don't let them dictate the terms of your friendship or keep you from socializing with others. These kinds of friends overwhelm us with their demands for time and attention, and can prevent us from forming bonds with others. Oftentimes we find ourselves doing what they want, rather than what we want, just for the sake of the friendship.

You can also have friends who don't respect your point of view and are apt to be overly judgmental. They keep you off balance by making you feel inferior or guilty. They are never wrong, and even when they are, you'll never get them to admit it. In defending themselves, they pull you down. Yes, their battle-ready stance has everything to do with how insecure they really are underneath the bravado, but don't expect them to acknowledge that, ever. You feel like no matter what you will say or do, you'll never come out on top or even on the same level, so you all too often overlook it and continue the circle of the irrational and wondrous entanglement referred to as "friendship." Don't spin your wheels.

Keep in mind the fact that people who are critical and judgmental have low self-esteem. Something in their past created a negative self-image that they're spending the present time defending against. This doesn't improve over time; in fact, it calcifies and dictates the kinds of relationships they'll have as adults. These so-called friends often disguise their emotions until something triggers the "true" person and elicits a negative response. Guilt, fear, criticism, and resentment are byproducts of low self-esteem, which some people disguise on a daily basis. Over time, you become closer and have more interaction, which sometimes permits the veil to come off and reveal the actual person.

A bona fide deal breaker is when you no longer trust your friend because of something he or she did or said. If he or she spilled one of your secrets or spoke maliciously about you behind your back, you have a legitimate reason to revoke your trust in him or her. For some people, that loss of trust may irreversibly affect the friendship, especially if they are only interested in themselves and their own problems and won't take the time to help with your tribulations while you help theirs. Whereas this lack of consideration could be a part of their personality, it's still inexcusably selfish and should be seen as a serious issue.

> Losing a friend hurts, but it hurts even more when a person causes you to lose your focus on what you want and, more importantly, who you are.

The moment of truth is deciding what to do. Do you want to maintain an acquaintanceship or completely cut the friend out of your life? You must meet this goat hunter head-on, realizing that your opinion may change after you confront your friend. Be open to that possibility going into the conversation. You absolutely and unequivocally must talk to your friend about how you feel. It will be tough to start this conversational ball rolling, but it must be done. Losing a friend hurts, but it hurts even more when someone causes you to lose your focus on what you want and, more importantly, who you are. When you finally sit down with this person, stay away from making personal attacks. Rather, coolly express your observations and concerns about your friend's behavior, and talk in terms of how your friend's actions have made you feel. Your friend can't defend your feelings. Talk openly and specifically about how your friend's hurtful actions have made you feel. Keep it focused on your feelings, not about blame. This is likely to make it easier for your friend to accept your criticism than if it's phrased as an attack on him or her or his or her actions.

On the other hand, if your friend does lose his or her cool and go into an angry catalogue of your misdeeds and infractions, sit back and hear him or her out, and then explain as calmly as you can that this is your time to air your grievances, and once you've finished with that and resolved them, you can move on to your friend's grievances. Don't be distracted, diverted, or bullied into backtracking. Say what you mean, and mean what you say.

> Sometimes we need to be able to live without something in order to have it. Once we can let go, we are in a position of greater power.

Realize as you're going through this that what's happened in the relationship is not just your friend's responsibility. You too are changing, growing, and realizing new things about yourself; you're resetting your limits, rethinking your needs, and may no longer be as tolerant as you were in the past about the behavior on your friend's part that now gets your goat. Do listen to what your friend has to say, once you've said your peace. He or she may have some points you hadn't considered. Most importantly, don't act in haste. A burned bridge is tough to recross, and if you later come to regret breaking off a friendship, you may well find it impossible to rebuild.

If, after consideration, you decide to try and repair this relationship, don't expect immediate results. Occasionally allowing a little fresh air between people is a good and healthy thing, and a cooling off period may be in order for both of you.

Sometimes we need to be able to live without something in order to have it. Once we can let go, we are in a position of greater power. Successful business people know that the only way to pull off a profitable deal is to become emotionally unattached.

LET THE COMPETITION BEGIN

Sibling rivalry is one of humanity's oldest problems, or for the purpose of this book and chapter, a huge "fence jumper." I'm talking about the competition that seems to spring up between brothers and sisters, brothers and brothers, or sisters and sisters, common to so many species. We compete for different things: food, territory, love, and attention. We pull each other's hair, yell about how the other guy is looking out our car window, and tattle on each other like there's no tomorrow. It's competition for what we as children perceive to be scarce resources we're unwilling to share, and it's the bane of parents in many families, not solely human. For most of us humans, the competition is for love, attention, and time.

Even at a young age, the capacity for emotional feeling is already rather well developed.

When I look at my wife and her brother, me and my brother, and now my two grandsons, it is easier to relate to the source of the problem. When my grandson Karter was born, all of his parents' available time and attention was only for him. Because of this, he feels rather special, and he's enjoyed spending over three years in these privileged circumstances. Even this limited period of time will have an enormous impact on Karter in his later life, and explains his only too natural resentment of the recent arrival of his younger brother, Kiptyn, aka The Intruder. As I recently observed Karter, he unconsciously looked for ways to irritate and bother Kiptyn. When his parents became aware of this, they reprimanded and punished Karter. However, this doesn't solve the problem. Punishing the older sibling simply makes him or her develop ways to retaliate that the parents won't be able to detect.

The root causes of sibling rivalry are the timeless and universal circumstances shared by all human families.

Some of you reading this who have never dealt with a sibling rivalry may believe that this is not possible. However, older children can be surprisingly creative, and according to most experts, the younger sibling has very little chance of winning this rivalry. In fact, the younger kid will most probably have a sense of continually losing to the older sib, and repeatedly experience all the frustration that creates. That said, not all younger siblings lose this fight; as they develop and wise up, they'll create tactics of their own to block their older sib's incursions and bother them as much as they themselves have been exasperated by their attacks. I want to emphasize that by no means is this a complete description of this complex problem. It is rather an attempt to point out the most important factors that contribute to this situation. There are many other factors that can affect rivalry, a difference in gender potentially being one of them. The fact is, no matter how evenhanded we try to be as parents, these rivalries have existed all through time as evidenced in mythology and fables common to all known cultures. These rivalries are one more reason it is important to be aware of what may mentally be stopping you. It is hard to keep your gate locked regarding this common occurrence within families. However, being more aware of its natural ebb and flow will reduce the chances of your goat getting loose.

BEWARE OF BOORISH BEHAVIOR

Ever wonder why some people delight in being rude? Before you let them bother you, consider this. They cannot be happy and be rude at the same time. There's just no way for mean and nice to work together in the same body. Their lives are entangled in a bevy of anger, disappointment, jealousy, discontent, and "what if's." They feed on negativity, communicate for the purpose of being heard, and have apologists to defend them. You've heard of the Stockholm Syndrome, in which hostages begin to identify with their captors? Well, it's not just for hostages. It means making excuses for the wrongdoer and is a behavior often seen in the friends of bullies, who go along with their powerful friends' mischief in order to avoid being the victims of it themselves. Challenging a bully can be dangerous and apologists find it easier to wimp out.

> Rude people want you to feel bad
> because they feel bad.

It's a rare friend who knows the value of being trustworthy and siding with you. Many people find it easier to selectively point out the logic in the abuser's position, like the abuser's right to free speech, for example. Rude people want you to feel bad because they feel bad. Being rude makes some people feel stronger. One reason why there are apologists: People tend to sympathize with those whose guilt they share. Thus, by shielding others' rudeness, they betray their own vested interest in not being blamed for having acted the same way. If you don't believe that anyone could find it in his heart to defend a rude person, just watch what happens when you tell someone how you stood up to the boorish person whose behavior seemed to you to be indefensible. Don't be surprised if someone calls you out—for rudeness!

Of course, whether they mean to or not, these defenders are just protecting the aggressor's interests. Watch and see who stands up for you in this situation. Those who do, really care.

THE DRAMA QUEEN

What is a drama queen? All of us experience conflicts and emotional upheavals as part of life, but for drama queens, these common setbacks can set off fireworks of operatic proportions. Everything the drama queen is going through is set in bold face letters; every twist and turn is blown up, exploited, and distorted in order to turn it into a major melodrama. Everything is a crisis, and the drama queen is always at the center of attention, or else.

Most of us can spot drama queens and learn to avoid them. Who needs the uproar? Most of us don't attempt to confront him or her (yes, they come in both genders), thus the drama queen may find himself or herself out of the social or political loop at work since their tendency to overreact or lash out at others irrationally makes it difficult for others to trust them with sensitive information.

While a drama queen might find her forceful personality and manipulation skills useful in a few situations, her inability to control her emotions and to form meaningful relationships always keeps her socially isolated.

From firsthand experience in dealing with a drama queen, I can tell you that these people are apt to be overbearing and to overreact to seemingly minor incidents. They have only two speeds, "off" and "off the chart." Their color wheel consists of black and white, and they live to amp up the wattage on any conflict they engage in. Throw in a dose of infantile behavior, and their worst fear is to be ignored or become powerless over others. While a drama queen might find her forceful personality and manipulation skills useful in a few situations, her inability to control her emotions and to form meaningful relationships always keeps her socially isolated. While those we love don't have to be exactly like us, life is too short for drama and petty things. Relationships aren't about whom you have known the longest, it's about those who came and never left your side. Remember, the next time you encounter a drama queen, gate your goat!

IS IT REAL OR IS IT MEMOREX?

For those who do not remember Memorex, it is the name of a manufacturer of recording tape used in VHS TV recorders before CDs, DVDs, and TiVo. Those of us who lived in the tape deck world still remember that great ad campaign line, "Is it real or is it Memorex?" The hook was that the product produced such a natural sound, you couldn't tell it from the live performance. Unfortunately, a lot of the people we encounter in our lives are as good at faking authenticity as Memorex was.

People who want to "fit in" employ self-presentation with their clothes, activities, and perceived status.

As Billy Sunday said, "Going to church doesn't make you a Christian any more than hanging out in a garage makes you a mechanic." Having children doesn't make you a mother or father. Having children makes you a parent who is responsible to become a mother or father and impact your children in a positive way. Saying "I love you" doesn't make you loyal and committed. Driving an expensive car doesn't mean you have money. Making excuses doesn't change the truth. So why do people masquerade around life trying to be something they are not?

Most people go through life not knowing who they are or what they want. People who want to "fit in" employ self-presentation with their clothes, activities, and perceived status. They settle, survive, and keep their heads down. This is easier than trying to be who they really are. Being real exposes you to vulnerability and judgment, which is scary. Life coach Elaine Bailey says, "Society creates a set of norms by which people are measured. When people are under pressure to fit in, they respond in a variety of ways. You want to keep the peace and hope they like you, so you say what you think they want to hear in order to become a people pleaser." You believe that your opinion is of lesser value and doesn't count. You perceive the other person's opinion is of far greater value. If you challenge or disagree with something, you'll be shot down or seen as difficult or negative. You want to be all the rage, but what does popularity mean if the friends surrounding you are just there for the person they perceive you to be, rather than who you really are under the hype? The lyric to the Trace Adkins song, *All Hat and No Cattle* says, "That boy just ain't real. All boots and no saddle … all hat and no cattle ain't gonna get it done." Sooner or later you're going to want to choose between being an everybody with a bunch of nobodies, or being a nobody with everybody who cares about you.

CLICK "UNFRIEND" TO BECOME HAPPIER

Do you have hundreds of friends—at least, on Facebook? Turns out that's not necessarily good for you, or at least for your level of life satisfaction. It's been reported in a recent study from Spain that Facebook users with over three hundred "friends" felt less satisfied with their lives after reading friends' status updates. However, those with fewer friends felt positive effects from reading their friends' status posts.

The explanation seems to be that we take what we see on Facebook at, er, face value, and assume that other's positive status posts reflect badly on our real (and less relentlessly upbeat) lives. The more the people around you seem to be thriving, the worse you feel about your own life.

The more buddies you have, the more brag posts you see, increasing the sense that other people are better off than you. Use your judgment to unsubscribe from contacts that might be making you feel less happy. Farewell, show-offs!

IMPOSSIBLE PEOPLE DO NO WRONG

Vampires are real—attention vampires, I mean. Do not permit yourself to get pulled into a relationship where your needs are constantly downgraded by theirs. It can be very draining.

The problem with an attention vampire is that nothing is ever enough. Everything is about them. It's their world, and you're just a bit player in the big picture. You can't reason with them, because their thirst for attention overwhelms every other consideration. Understand that it's not you, it's them. This can be surprisingly difficult, considering that this kind of impossible person is a past master at shifting the blame. Chances are, the more often they blame you, the more they are actually at fault.

However you got into this unhappy relationship, drive a stake into it as soon as you can. Don't make it about blame; blame is what they do, and they have a lot more practice. If you're worried that you might be the problem, you almost certainly are not.

Impossible people are good at seeming normal. So good at it, in fact, that you might be tempted in a weak moment to let them back into your life. Don't do it. Invariably, they will bring that confidence back to haunt you, using it as a weapon and a wedge. They're ruthless, manipulative, and in their own minds, always right. Somehow, they will find a way to use your mistaken attempt at reconciliation to make you look bad and make themselves look better. They can't help it—but you can. Cut them loose, and don't look back.

BUILD YOUR FENCE

Understand that eventually, you'll have to create a separation between yourself and people that hunt your goat. Whether they are a friend, a family member, a parent, even a spouse, the time to leave will eventually manifest itself. Maintaining relationships with people who try to get your goat is literally impossible. If you can't, or won't, make a physical departure immediately, make a mental one. In your mind, you've already left the relationship. The only thing left to do is wait for physical reality to reflect that fact.

Avoid becoming what you loathe. If you aren't careful, you could *find yourself* adopting much of the goat hunter's own behavior, even if you aren't voluntarily trying. Eschew blame entirely by understanding that this is just the way the other person is. These things define their actions, and nothing you do can change any part of their past. Be the opposite of them: a possible person. Live as an example of tolerance, patience, humility, and even some kindness, as difficult as that may be. We are all influenced by the people in our environment and they don't have to be perfect all the time and neither do you. Give respect because you are human. If you don't receive respect, that's sadly their problem. Ultimately, this sort of behavior is probably the only thing that might get through to them. They may not change in everything, but you can safely expect a change.

> There comes a time in your life, when
> you walk away from all the drama
> and people who create it.

It is always our choice whether we get on with our life and live based on who we are instead of chaining ourselves to people who hold grudges and are not enriching. Be an active participant, not someone whose choices are handed to them. You owe unkind or unthinking people no loyalty, and no reasonable code of conduct holds you to them. If the relationship is a rock chained to your leg, are you really required by loyalty to go jump in the lake?

Try putting your own needs and considerations first. Part of maturing as a human being is knowing when it's time to walk away from the unreasonable expectations of others, and get on with it. Find people who make you happy, and who you make happy in turn;

people you can confide in, laugh with, and love without fear. Focus on the good in yourself and in others, love the people who treat you right, and pray for the ones who don't. You may feel guilty, but if you know you made the right decision for yourself, stand by it. Life is too short to be anything but happy.

Exercise Your Goat

The Power to Change
What Holds You Back

Most of us know by now that we should be exercising on a regular basis. Do you really know why exercise is so important? Not only does working out help you shed a few pounds, but there are also many other compelling reasons to include some regular physical activity in your routine.

Exercise can help you sleep better, reduce your stress, and improve your intellectual clarity. It allows us to feel different about ourselves. The same can be said of mental exercise. Exercising our goat promotes a healthy immune system necessary to overcoming what sometimes gets in our way and inevitably holds us back. Exercise will tone our minds and allow us to focus our thinking on what will take us to the next level. One thing that holds people back from realizing their full potential is their own mind. Your internal brain chatter replays over and over in the subconscious mind.

Most people go through life not even aware of this internal processing, which directly affects their external actions and decisions, which results in their external conditions. You get stuck in your ways and anything that diverts you from your routines, plans, and comfort zone, can be very annoying. Worse yet, life's diversions are sometimes unsettling and painful.

Every health and wellness expert says the same thing. To be healthy isn't just about eating the right food; you have to exercise.

FIRST THINGS FIRST

In *The Road Less Traveled*, M. Scott Peck includes a telling story about himself and his personal ineptitude in fixing things. Anytime he attempted to make minor repairs or put something together, the result was always confusion, failure, and frustration. One day on a walk, he saw a neighbor repairing a lawn mower. Peck told the man, "Boy, I sure admire you. I've never been able to fix those kinds of things or do anything like that." "That's because you don't take the time," the neighbor answered. After reflecting on the man's statement, Peck decided to test its truth. The next time he faced a mechanical challenge, he took his time and focused his attention on the problem. Much to his surprise, at age thirty-seven, he succeeded. After that, he knew he was not "cursed or genetically defective or otherwise incapacitated or impotent." If he wanted to go to the next level in that area of his life, he could do it if he was willing to mentally focus on it.

Focus on what brings you the highest reward, what you enjoy most and do the best.

James Allen said, "You will become as small as your controlling desire, as great as your dominant aspiration." A large number of people are simply okay with where they are without realizing that is what holds them back. They are like the small sea plankton that goes wherever the current takes it. You must take into account your priorities and set your own agenda for your life. Living your life without priorities exposes your goat to extraneous distractions that can hold you back. Removing distractions is no small matter in our culture, but it is critical because, as W. Clement Stone says, you can "keep your mind off the things you don't want by keeping it on the things you do want." I've heard it said that "many people land on priorities based on where they run out of steam." When that happens, other people are planning your life.

To avoid this, begin by focusing on your strengths, the things that make best use of your skills and God-given talents. You might also focus on what brings you the highest reward, what you enjoy most and do the best. The Pareto principle (also known as the 80–20 rule, the law of the vital few, and the principle of factor scarcity) states that, for many events, roughly 80 percent of the effects come from 20 percent of the causes. It is beneficial to apply the Pareto principle to your priorities by placing 80 percent of your effort on the top 20 percent of your activities. Give your attention to the areas that bear fruit. It takes discipline to practice your priorities. Start by choosing to do first things first: the activities that give you the highest return. That way you keep the distractions to a minimum.

INCONVENIENCE IS A PART OF LIFE

As Catholic priest John Powell said, "Many of us, unfortunately, feel like a floating boat at the mercy of the winds and waves. We have no ballast when the winds rage and the waves churn. We say things like, 'He made me so mad.' 'You really get me.' 'Her remark embarrassed me terribly.' 'The weather really depresses me.' 'This job really bores me.' 'The very sight of him saddens me.' We are content to blame others for our circumstances. The fully human person, as Shake-speare puts it in Julius Caesar, knows that, 'The fault, dear Brutus, Is not with our stars, but with ourselves.'"

Let's face it; your car is going to get dented, someone will hit your mailbox, the plumbing will spring a leak, and traffic will make you late for that big meeting. A whole succession of small vexing personal inconveniences will come in waves and are a normal part of life. Learning to roll with them is the best we can hope for, since perfection isn't possible in this world.

In the midst of your heartbreak, anxiety, and despair, you are being recreated.

You must build up your immune system to accept the circum-stances you face on a daily basis, and more significantly, grow from them. Sometimes you don't realize the lessons you are being taught because you are focused on the wrong thing. In the midst of your heartbreak, anxiety, and despair, you are being recreated. You are finding qualities of your being that you never knew existed. Remember, these conditions will either make you bitter or better, stronger or weaker. Don't forget them when the problems are solved. But the next time you are overwhelmed with misfortunes, you won't have to ask, why? You will know you are approaching a time of discovery. The power to change can sometimes require persistent workouts that involve exercises you need to do on a regular basis to hide your goat.

LOVE UNCONDITIONALLY

Think of love as an action, not a feeling. What is unconditional love? More to the point, let's define what it isn't: If you have to do something special, or act in a particular way to earn it, or if it's a love that can be taken away if you don't measure up, it's not unconditional. Start thinking of love as how you act, not what others do; it's a feeling you can generate for yourself based on your own behavior. Thus, it becomes a self-perpetuating act of generosity. As Stephanie Dowrick says, "love is not love except when it is generous." Feelings cannot last, but you can renew them continuously with new actions.

MAINTAIN A SENSE OF YOUTHFUL ENTHUSIASM

Jonathan Wells says, "If you want to feel old at any age, all you need to do is convince yourself that your best days are in the past." Do you feel that way about your life? I hope not, because nothing is more likely to sap your vigor than the certainty your best days have passed, or diminish your hopeful attitude toward the future than your conviction that you no longer play an active part in making it happen.

Get ahold of that attitude and take control of it. How many times have you heard someone say that today is all we have? They were right, but it's hard to hold onto that knowledge when so much of life seems dedicated to distracting us from that essential truth. Reaffirm your youth by taking back youth's optimistic view of your life and future. Someday, you'll look back on *these* as the good old days, so why wait? Possibilities abound; all it takes is the eyes to see them. Life is like that old ad line about the lottery; you have to be in it to win it. Be in your life as fully as you can.

HAVE HOPE IN HOPELESS SITUATIONS

Why do some people remain so upbeat, even though they experience things that you and I may never experience in our lifetimes? They never give up hope. At a moment when everything appears hopeless, you have two options. Option number one is to hold a pity party and get angry. Option number two is to remember that our hope produces endurance. Hope produces perseverance. When you know that there is a detailed plan and purpose for your life, you are going to endure the difficulties and you are going to have hope in hopeless situations. Hope is a decision and is a statement of faith. Faith believes in things when common sense tells you not to.

NURTURE YOUR SOUL BY GIVING

One of my favorite stories is about the woman who took her children to a restaurant and her six-year-old son asked if he could say grace. As they bowed their heads he said, "God is good. God is great. Thank you for the food, and I would even thank you more if Mom gets us ice cream for dessert. And liberty and justice for all! Amen!" Along with the laughter from the other customers nearby, the mother and her son heard a woman remark, "That's what's wrong with this country. Kids today don't even know how to pray. Asking God for ice cream! Unbelievable!" The boy burst into tears and asked his mother, "Did I do it wrong? Is God mad at me?" As his mother held him and assured him that he had done a terrific job and God was certainly not mad at him, an elderly gentleman approached the table. He winked at the boy and said, "I happen to know that God thought that was a great prayer." "Really?" the boy asked. "Cross my heart," the man replied. Then, in a theatrical whisper, he added, pointing to the woman whose remark had started this whole thing, "Too bad she never asks God for ice cream. A little ice cream is good for the soul sometimes." Naturally, the mother bought her kids ice cream at the end of the meal. Her son stared at his for a moment and then did something she would remember the rest of her life. He picked up his sundae and, without a word, walked over and placed it in front of the woman. With a big smile he told her, "Here, this is for you. Ice cream is good for the soul sometimes, and my soul is good already." Sometimes we all need some ice cream.

UNDERSTAND THE IMPORTANCE OF FORGIVENESS

Mahatma Gandhi said, "The weak can never forgive. Forgiveness is the attribute of the strong." We all tend to think of forgiving as something we have to extend to others who have wronged us. It may surprise you to find out that the hardest person to forgive is yourself. Why is that so? Maybe you've got a lot invested in your self-blame and self-hatred. Maybe a lot of your personal identity is built on that hard rock. Sure, it's familiar territory; it's the world you know. But it's a pretty harsh place to live in. Is the perception of the security it gives you reason enough to put up with the pain and discomfort it imposes on you? I don't think so. All that inner-directed anger has a price, and you won't know how much you've paid already until you're able to forgive yourself and to shed it. Embrace forgiveness, even when it seems impossible. More impossible is the task of living in a state of being unable to forgive; one in which you're consumed by fear of your vulnerability, inflamed by anger and pain, and carrying the load of guilt and regrets. You can do better things with the energy that's required to haul that load of useless misery on your shoulders. Feed your soul, not your negativity. The future belongs to those with the strength to lift their eyes to the possible, not those who are always looking back over their shoulder at a past they can't change.

STAY IN THE GAME

Calvin Coolidge said, "Nothing in the world, including talent, genius and education, can take the place of persistence." An unknown poet put it another way; "When the funds are low and the debts are high, don't quit. When things go wrong, and I can promise you they will, don't quit!"

Perseverance is a day-by-day decision not to give up. When we feel lost, overwhelmed, betrayed, or exhausted, we need to know we have a choice for how we respond. At the lowest point in my life I will always remember my best friend saying to me, "The only way to make a 'come back' is to go on." The first half of my life didn't go exactly as planned and I took some vicious hits. Divorce, not enough time for my kids, guilt, and loneliness were a few of the pains

I endured. Like many people, I started my life with good intentions but got blindsided along the way. I started to wonder if this was really as good it gets and then I realized, just as in my favorite sport of football, there was a second half. I had the power to change and overcome what may have been holding me back. Regardless of where you are, don't settle for life on its own terms.

POSSESS YOUR POSSESSIONS

Look forward to new horizons and possess your possessions. If you were a farmer you could say that a field was your possession. To possess that field you would have to work the land, plow it, weed it, fertilize it, and plant it. If you had the gift of a singing voice you could claim singing as your possession. To possess that gift you would have to practice, seek out an instructor, and train your voice to sing correctly. Learn all you can, be all you can, train all you can, and do all you can. If you want to control it, own it, and have power over it, then possess it. It's time to exercise your goat and overcome what is holding you back.

IT'S ALL GOOD

Conflict is neither good nor bad so don't let it hold you back. Conflict offers the opportunity to learn. As Kenneth Kaye says, "If necessity is the mother of invention, conflict is its father." Conflict can provide an opportunity for personal growth. The Chinese symbol for conflict is a combination of two Chinese words: danger and opportunity. This symbol provides a neutral label for conflict. You may find it helpful to think of conflict as neither positive nor negative. Conflict doesn't mean there's an impending disaster but includes a possible positive opportunity. Dealing with continual change creates tension, stress and anxiety. Multiply that times the number of people in a particular situation and tension develops, patience runs short, people lose sight of the bigger picture and become self-focused. All of this causes conflict and holds us back.

AN EXERCISE IN FUTILITY

When you're feeling overwhelmed or rejected, or if you have excessive stress in your life, it will manifest itself in a number of ways. It is important to pay attention when this happens and deal with what's going on. Sometimes, in the midst of difficulties, you can get so caught up in the situation you aren't even aware of how it is affecting you. A great example of this is complaining. Instead of being grateful for what you have and all the blessings that have been imparted on you, you focus on the current circumstances and fall into the trap of complaining. It isn't easy to stay away from being pessimistic when things go wide of the mark. However, complaining is an unhelpful practice.

> Complaining is truly an exercise in futility because half the people don't care about your problem, and the others are just glad you have the problem instead of them.

It's common for anyone to complain occasionally, but when your complaints escalate and your perspective turns critical, you have fallen into a toxic situation. Complaining is truly an exercise in futility because half the people don't care about your problem, and the others are just glad you have the problem instead of them. More importantly, complaining is self-destructive because your mind is continually occupied with negative thoughts. Figure out why you're complaining so much. Is it because of the circumstances in your life? Often what you're complaining about is not really what's bothering you. If you have a chronic feeling of dissatisfaction and constantly complain, take a hard look at what's really going on. That way you break the complaining habit and clear your mind for more positive and productive thoughts.

EXERCISE SELF-CONTROL

When emotion is directed inward, it is fear. When emotion is directed outward, it is anger. Both of these emotions are reactions to people or situations that you choose. This is not rocket science but, rather, very basic. Your feelings arise from thoughts that you choose. Therefore, you choose your feelings.

Beyond our primary needs for food, clothing, and shelter, there are three other needs we all share. Every person wants to feel important and valued. As a child, you needed to be loved. As you grow older, you need to be loved, valued and appreciated. None of us ever outgrow our basic human need for love. This basic need may emerge when we feel left out, or when we believe we have something valuable to contribute and no one asks our opinion.

We all need to be in control of our lives. Unfortunately, the clock controls a great deal of our life, other people's expectations, and schedules determined by everyone from our boss to our spouse. As a person who is on an airplane several times a week, I am at the mercy of someone else's control. I have a strong need to control every aspect of my life, and when I can't, my goat pokes it head out to take a peek. Additionally, you need to feel good about yourself. A sense of self-worth is the foundation of self-confidence, and the greater your self-confidence, the greater your ability to control anger and conflict. Whenever you feel threatened, or your need to feel good about yourself and be in control seems endangered, you may react emotionally with fear or anger.

> ## People can't get your goat if you don't tell them where it's tied.

Many people today want everything yesterday and expect the ultimate in quality. They have unreasonable requests with deadlines that are unrealistic. Anyone who works in the world of customer service can tell you that if you are going to keep customers happy and yourself sane, you'd better have vast stores of self-control. Some people have been put on this earth to get your goat, to push your buttons, and to make you lose control. It is time to exercise and hide your goat. People can't get your goat if you don't tell them where it's tied. Letting others "get your goat" puts them in control. We are ultimately giving them tremendous power over us. Staying in control is a learned skill and must be part of your daily mental exercise routine.

REACTIONS PRODUCE OUTCOMES

You choose your reaction in any situation. Your reaction will either hold you back, or be what catapults you forward. Your reactions are not forced on you by circumstances over which you have no power. The manner in which you respond to a situation will dictate the outcome. In essence, you need to determine what outcome you want. How do you react when you feel afraid or when you feel angry? You will most likely respond by retaliating, dominating, isolating yourself, or coping. Coping is the path that will free you, while the other three reactions will hold you back.

When you react to conflict by coping, you will always keep your goat hidden from other people.

When you decide to get even, to "get back" at someone, you not only expose your goat, you basically offer it up to be found, untied, and ridden down the street. As a child, you hit your brother or sister, or told your parents what they did wrong. Retaliation is a reaction that takes place at home, work, and play. People retaliate by gossiping, ignoring, and ostracizing. Some people respond to situations by domination. They resort to yelling, screaming, and swearing. Children call each other names, as do adults. Other people dominate through their job titles, intellectual superiority, or even their physical stature. Retaliation and domination are predominant among "type A" personalities, while isolation is the preferred response of a person who is more passive than aggressive.

Some people react to situations by withdrawing, sulking, or pouting. My brother and I were great examples. He tended to withdraw and pout, while I chose to get even or dominate the situation. Of course, the preferable path to take in every situation is to work out the problems, first with yourself, and then with other people. When you entail your skills to effectively manage a situation, the outcome allows you to get beyond what may hold other people back. When you react to conflict by coping, you will always keep your goat hidden from other people.

MANAGE YOUR DIFFERENCES

One of your ongoing exercises needs to be focused around building the kind of relationships that make for a happier and more productive life. Norman Vincent Peale said, "Avoid argument, but when a negative attitude is expressed, counter with a positive and optimistic comment." All too often, instead of managing our differences when a problem arises, we are too quick to attack the person instead of the problem. When this occurs, the gates are unlocked and two people's goats run wild and usually lock horns. When you fail to distinguish between the behavior and the person, it isn't just counterproductive; it is destructive. If you want to keep your goat behind the gate, exercise your ability to address the particular behavior, not the individual's personality. Attacking people's characters is never going to get them to change their behavior or attitude. Conversely, it will make them become defensive and closed-minded regarding anything you suggest they need to change.

To get past what is holding you back requires exercising new options to move you forward.

When something goes wrong, don't get stuck justifying your position and defending yourself. Be willing to give up some ground. To get past what is holding you back requires exercising new options to move you forward. When problems arise, instead of explaining or justifying your behavior, focus on finding a solution to the problem.

On more than one occasion, the person who is scheduled to introduce me at an event has said, "By the way, do you have a formal introduction? I never received one from your office." The fact is, we always e-mail the meeting planner my introduction, and record the date, time, and recipient in our event details. We know exactly when it was received and opened. Instead of blaming them, or worse yet, throwing my program manager under the bus, I reply, "No worries; it probably got trapped in your spam and you never saw it. If we can find a computer with a printer, I will print out a copy for you." I now actually carry extra copies to avoid finding a computer and printer. For the record, that used to really get my goat.

STOP TALKING ABOUT IT

A good friend of mine has been in the hair salon business for over 25 years. He is a very good stylist. However, he is an incredible artist. Four of his paintings hang in our home. Even more remarkable is the fact he spends virtually all of his time styling hair instead of painting. Why? Only he can answer that question. As I have said to him before, "You do not get a practice life. You will get one shot here on earth to wake up every day and share your passion and gift of painting." So what exactly is holding him back?

Many people know in their heart what they would wake up and do every day if they knew they wouldn't fail, but that fear of failing holds them back. When you are afraid of failing, you become tempted to do nothing. To get beyond your "relative success" you have to take risks. Don't overanalyze to the point of paralysis. That is a form of avoidance. You put your energy into thinking instead of acting. Grasping at straws is when you find yourself wishing and hoping that your circumstances could be different. Restart your wishes as specific goals. Don't let wishing be a substitute for real actions. When you are caught wishing, you often believe you are doing more than you really are.

Every day is a new day.

Stop abandoning your dreams because of your fear of being judged harshly on the final project. For me, I sometimes struggle to move forward because of my perfectionist tendencies. I am forever trying to continually improve it and make the final product perfect, and too many times have let things get my goat because of my self-defeating behavior. Every day is a new day. Even if you have to go back to square one, go ahead and feel frustrated but don't feel helpless and totally defeated. Most coaches tell their players that win or lose, the game is over once we shower and walk out that door. You will never win the next time you play if you're thinking about the last time you lost. Stop talking about your dreams and passions and worrying about what might go wrong. You're going to have some hiccups. So hold your breath, count to five, and keep moving forward.

DON'T WAIT TO BE HAPPY

Many of us continue to postpone our happiness indefinitely because of our inability to hide our goat. We live under the false facade that someday when the bills are paid, the children are raised, and we live in a bigger house and drive a nicer car, we will be happy. Meanwhile, life keeps moving forward. Your life will always be filled with challenges. Not until you finally admit this to yourself, and decide to be happy anyway, will you ever completely hide your goat. Life doesn't magically begin when the car is paid off, when you get married, or when you get a promotion at work. Don't live your entire life waiting for it to begin. In my book *Enjoy the Ride* I challenge people to live more for today, less for tomorrow, and never about yesterday. The reality is that someone, or something, will always be trying to get your goat. Hiding your goat is not the way to happiness. Happiness is the way to hide your goat.

QUICK REFERENCE GUIDE

To Hide Your Goat ...

Understand Where Negativity Begins

⇨ abandonment: feeling unwanted

⇨ no stability: irresponsibility

⇨ no limits: inability to say no

⇨ avoidance: need to be liked outweighs need to confront

⇨ discipline: control or out of control

⇨ attention: needs excitement, chaos, or drama

Realize How Negativity Is Developed

⇨ biology

⇨ genetics

⇨ existing physiological characteristics

⇨ environment

⇨ caught and taught behaviors

⇨ parents or parental figures

⇨ role models, friends, and idols

⇨ cultural conditioning

⇨ societal values

⇨ training and education

⇨ experiences

⇨ past and present circumstances

⇨ personal choices

⇨ behaviors, decisions, and beliefs

⇨ constructive choices: responsible and helpful

⇨ unconstructive choices: irresponsible and harmful

Recognize Why Negativity Continues

⇨ Habitual thinking makes it normal to focus on wrong

⇨ Cultures accept it

⇨ We tolerate it

⇨ Sensationalism sells

⇨ It naively elevates self-esteem

⇨ It subtly gets in

⇨ It gets attention

Identify What Negativity Costs

⇨ productivity

⇨ substandard performance

⇨ morale

⇨ deadlines aren't met

⇨ quality

⇨ mistakes increase

⇨ average is accepted

⇨ confidence is lost

⇨ wasted resources

⇨ time

⇨ money

How to Change Your Behavior

⇨ Be willing to learn and grow

⇨ Be aware of the need for change

⇨ Have the incentive to change

⇨ Be committed to change

⇨ Have a realistic plan for changing

⇨ Foster support and encouragement

⇨ Be accountable

⇨ Foster constructive feedback on progress

⇨ Appreciate opportunities to learn from mistakes

⇨ Be mindful of the consequences of continued noncompliance

How to Influence Other People's Behavior

⇨ Show you have an authentic desire to be helpful and care

⇨ Make them aware by discussing the issues openly and honestly

⇨ Actively listen with interest and understand without condoning or judging

⇨ Evaluate existing choices and possible constructive alternatives and the consequences of continuing old behavior

⇨ Explore what people are willing to change and if they are willing to take responsibility for making changes

⇨ Focus on problems, not people

⇨ Be honest

⇨ Assume the best about people

⇨ Practice patience and self-control

⇨ Constructively express your feelings

How to Adjust Your Outlook

⇨ Avoid negative relationships

⇨ Minimize the negative information you take in on a daily basis

⇨ Maintain a childlike innocence

⇨ Accept life on life's terms

⇨ Guard your self-talk

⇨ Let go of the negatives from your past

How To Cultivate Richer Relationships

⇨ Be vulnerable and admit your fears and shortcomings

⇨ Stop making negative assumptions

⇨ Stop being so critical

⇨ Get more involved by caring enough to know and knowing enough to care

⇨ Be willing to be the first to change

How to Become More Enjoyable to Be Around

⇨ Apologize when appropriate

⇨ Be willing to talk about issues

⇨ Acknowledge other people's viewpoints

⇨ Recognize good points

⇨ Always be fair and equitable

⇨ Practice participation, not dictation

⇨ Think of what they want

⇨ Respect their perception

⇨ Don't argue your opinion

How to Set the Right Example

⇨ Always deal with the facts

⇨ Practice being outstanding

⇨ Communicate openly and honestly

⇨ Match your actions to your beliefs

What Are the Reasons for Conflict?

⇨ personality differences

⇨ organizational culture

⇨ values

⇨ goals

⇨ job descriptions

⇨ perception

⇨ communication

⇨ baggage

⇨ policies and procedures

⇨ available resources

How to Cope with Conflict

⇨ Control your emotions during a confrontation

⇨ Make decisions based on accurate and complete information and not solely on the opinions of others

⇨ Do not deliver ultimatums prematurely whenever a problem arises in an effort to solve it quickly

⇨ Don't ignore the problem hoping it will eventually go away

⇨ Don't assume the problem is an isolated occurrence

⇨ Focus on what is right, not who is right

What Can Cause You Stress

⇨ complaining that nothing is ever right

⇨ not being able to make decisions

⇨ being inflexible and rejecting anything new

⇨ disorganization

⇨ being self-centered and unable to handle criticism

⇨ blaming others or circumstances for your problems

⇨ playing the role of the victim

⇨ being impatient and wanting everything now

⇨ eating, drinking, and smoking too much, or using stimuli that can be destructive if not moderated

Be Aware of the Most Common Stress-Producing Circumstances

⇨ perfectionism

⇨ guilt

⇨ change

⇨ relationships

⇨ finances

⇨ job

Create a Daily Checklist to Reduce Stress

⇨ Go to bed early and become a morning person

⇨ Eat a well-balanced diet to stay energized

⇨ Take a walk to maintain your metabolism

⇨ Spend ten minutes of quiet time to reboot your brain

⇨ Take your breaks and lunch hours

⇨ Do something fun and play

⇨ Try something new and learn to let go

⇨ Set limits and learn to say no

⇨ Go home on time and never forget what's important

⇨ Have a support person to keep you encouraged

⇨ Handle the truth

⇨ Assign the right value to circumstances

⇨ Be honest in everything

Stay Internally Balanced

⇨ Expose your mind to constructive inputs

⇨ Emotionally process and express feelings rationally and constructively

⇨ Physically exercise and eat a balanced diet

⇨ Love yourself and others in harmony with your life and cultivate a depth of wisdom and correctness in your beliefs

Stay Externally Balanced

⇨ family

⇨ work

⇨ play

⇨ relationships

⇨ social life

⇨ financial

⇨ activities

Understand the Importance of Stimulus

Stimulus for the most part comes from two sources: people and information. It is important to surround yourself with the right people and consume good information. Your primary stimuli produce your thoughts.

Thoughts interact with our emotional and physical system to produce actions. Constructive thoughts lead to constructive actions. In this context, constructive means responsible, self-developing, and mature. The word unconstructive means irresponsible, self-defeating, and immature.

Actions tend to be consistent with our thoughts. Inconsistencies may be controlled by subconscious thoughts, our emotions, or our physical system and tend to result in inner tension. Actions that are practiced become habits. Constructive actions lead to constructive habits.

Habits are practiced thoughts, feelings, and actions. Our habits shape our character. Constructive habits lead to the development of a healthy, strong character.

Character is our mental, emotional, physical, and spiritual characteristics as a whole person. Our character shapes our life path.

Life Path is long-term behavioral patterns, our life style (including our priorities, goals, and activities), and our destiny as a winner or loser. A change in character will produce a change in our life path by affecting our behavioral patterns, life style, or destiny.

FINAL THOUGHT

While most of us spend a substantial quantity of our existence hiding our goat, it is important to point out that we should also be shepherds to others in their pursuit to hide their goats. More than 25 years ago I reported to a gentleman who helped me hide my goat and has remained a great friend. He was forever challenging me to stay balanced, set the right example to people, and develop constructive habits that would enhance me personally and professionally. Within the plethora of files and my overabundance of notes that I referenced to write this book, I came across something he wrote to me when I was his subordinate. I will always remember the kind words and encouraging notes he periodically gave me. On one occasion, he left an inspirational article on my desk with the following handwritten note attached to it.

Steve,

This article has been very helpful to me. Maybe it will be useful in your personal and spiritual life. Don't read too much into it; it is not coming from Mark the manager, but from Mark who wants to see you be a success in life. I have never been around a more talented, thought-provoking and creative individual. The sky is the limit for you. You have the potential for greatness. Stay focused and let God be your guide.

—Mark

I am extremely grateful to all of the shepherds who blessed me with their extraordinary wisdom and knowledge. This book is a tribute to their good judgment and insight. Over the years, many people have supplied me with a wealth of inspiring information. I am indebted to the various authors, speakers, seminar leaders, trainers, and colleagues who have influenced my writing over the better part of three decades. To those of you who have sent me articles after hearing me speak, and simply said, "I thought you might enjoy reading this," thank you for helping me put in writing...*Hide Your Goat!*

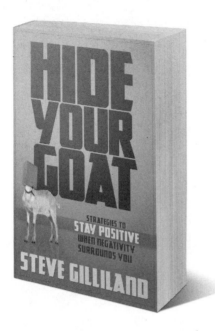

How can you use this book?

MOTIVATE

EDUCATE

THANK

INSPIRE

PROMOTE

CONNECT

Why have a custom version of *Hide Your Goat?*

⇨ Build personal bonds with customers, prospects, employees, donors, and key constituencies

⇨ Develop a long-lasting reminder of your event, milestone, or celebration

⇨ Provide a keepsake that inspires change in behavior and change in lives

⇨ Deliver the ultimate "thank you" gift that remains on coffee tables and bookshelves

⇨ Generate the "wow" factor

Books are thoughtful gifts that provide a genuine sentiment that other promotional items cannot express. They promote employee discussions and interaction, reinforce an event's meaning or location, and they make a lasting impression. Use your book to say "Thank You" and show people that you care.

Hide Your Goat is available in bulk quantities and in customized versions at special discounts for corporate, institutional, and educational purposes. To learn more please contact our Special Sales team at:

1.866.775.1696 • sales@advantageww.com • www.AdvantageSpecialSales.com

OTHER BOOKS FROM HALL OF FAME SPEAKER AND BESTSELLING AUTHOR STEVE GILLILAND

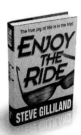

Enjoy The Ride

This book focuses on you the individual and is a blueprint for getting the most out of life. It's an eye-opening book that causes people to examine where they are personally and professionally. It lifts people up and inspires them to evolve and appreciate rather than simply maintain and exist. If you want to achieve true success and fulfillment, you must first discover an enthusiasm for your work and personal life. Decide where you are heading, get on the bus, choose the right seat and *Enjoy The Ride*™!

Hardcover —103 pages

Making a Difference

This book lays out three manageable means to positively influence people in every imaginable way, regardless of our position or status. It is about the conscious choices we make every day that impact the lives of others. While we don't always know what challenges face the people we meet every day, we do have the power to bring them hope. That hope can multiply a thousand times over and spread exponentially. This is the essential, motivating truth behind *Making a Difference*™.

Hardcover —190 pages